I0488362

Clarity Emerging

The paintings of
Christopher Michael Creath

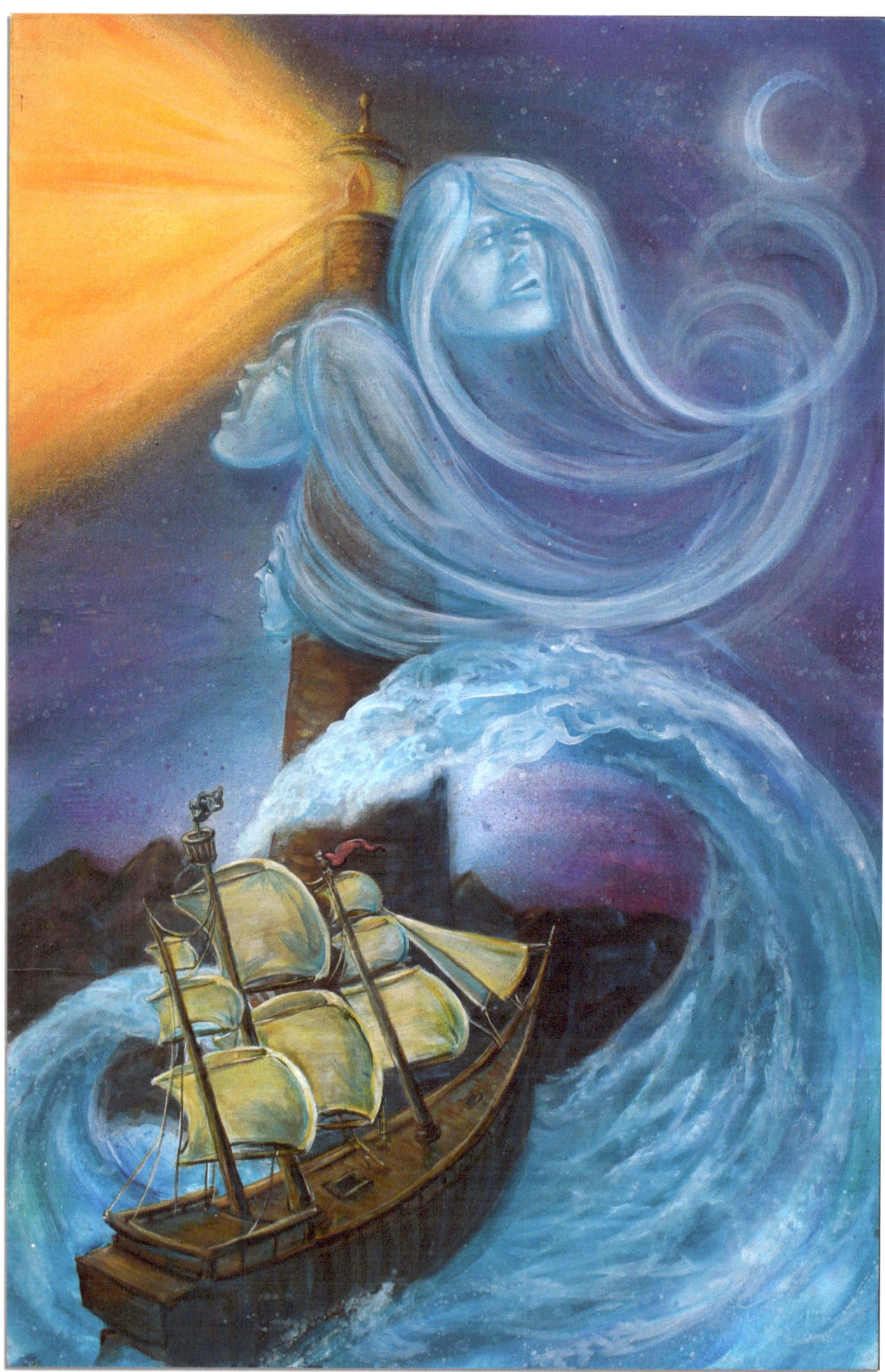

Siren Song 36"x24"

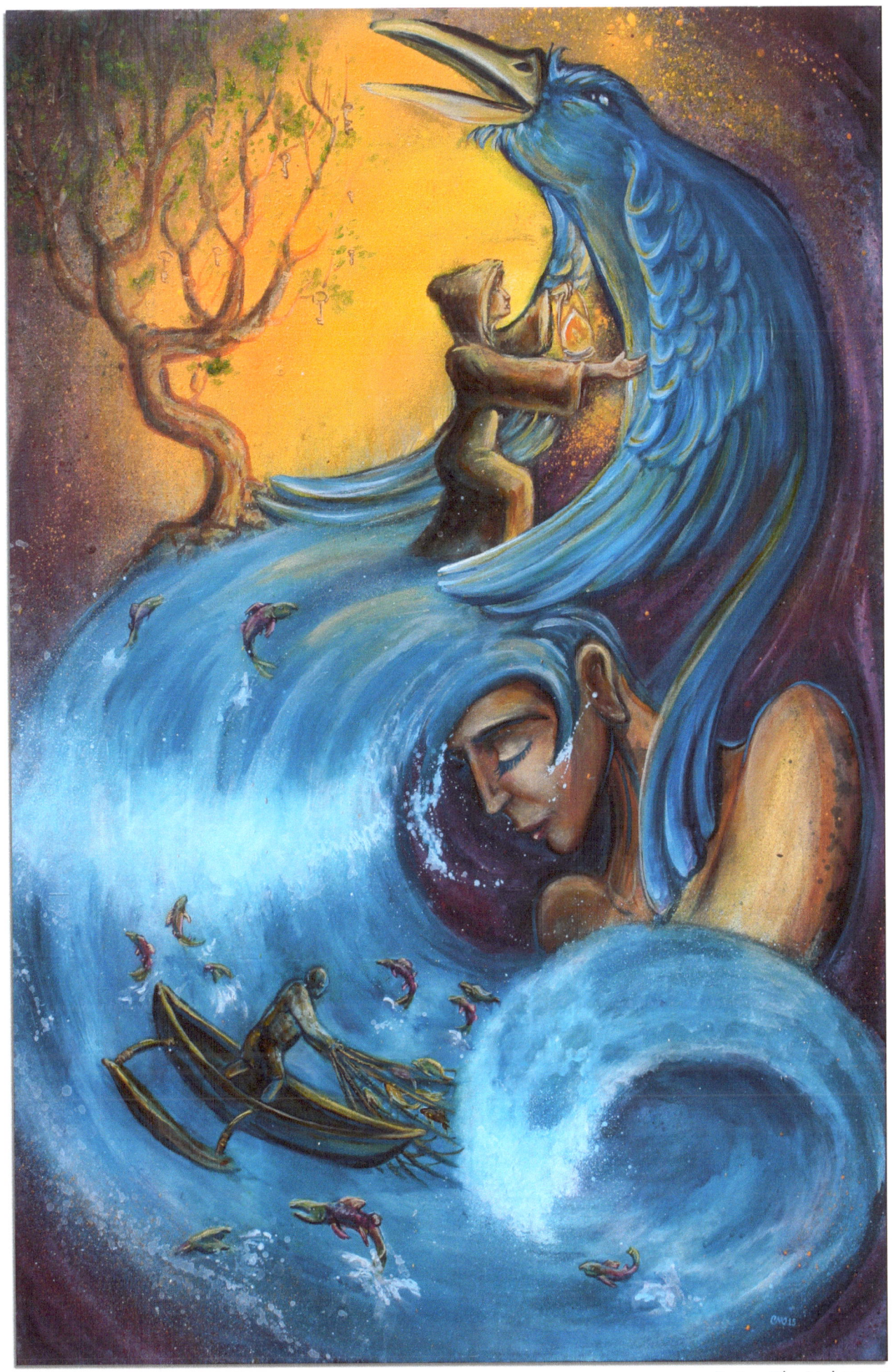

Parting The Veil 36"x24"

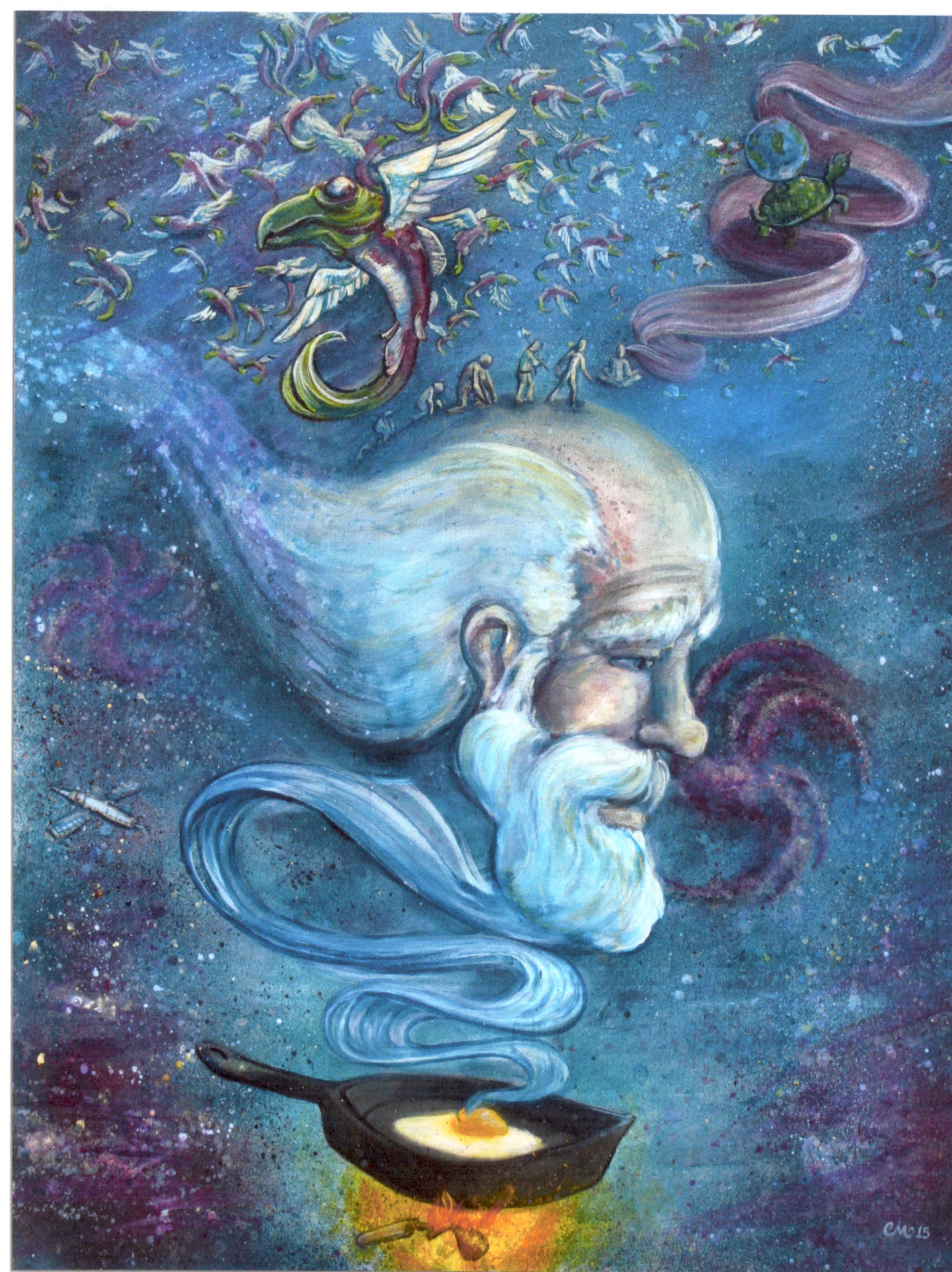

Darwin Emanating from a Fried Egg Appeared to me in Some Mildew on my Bathtub 24"x36"

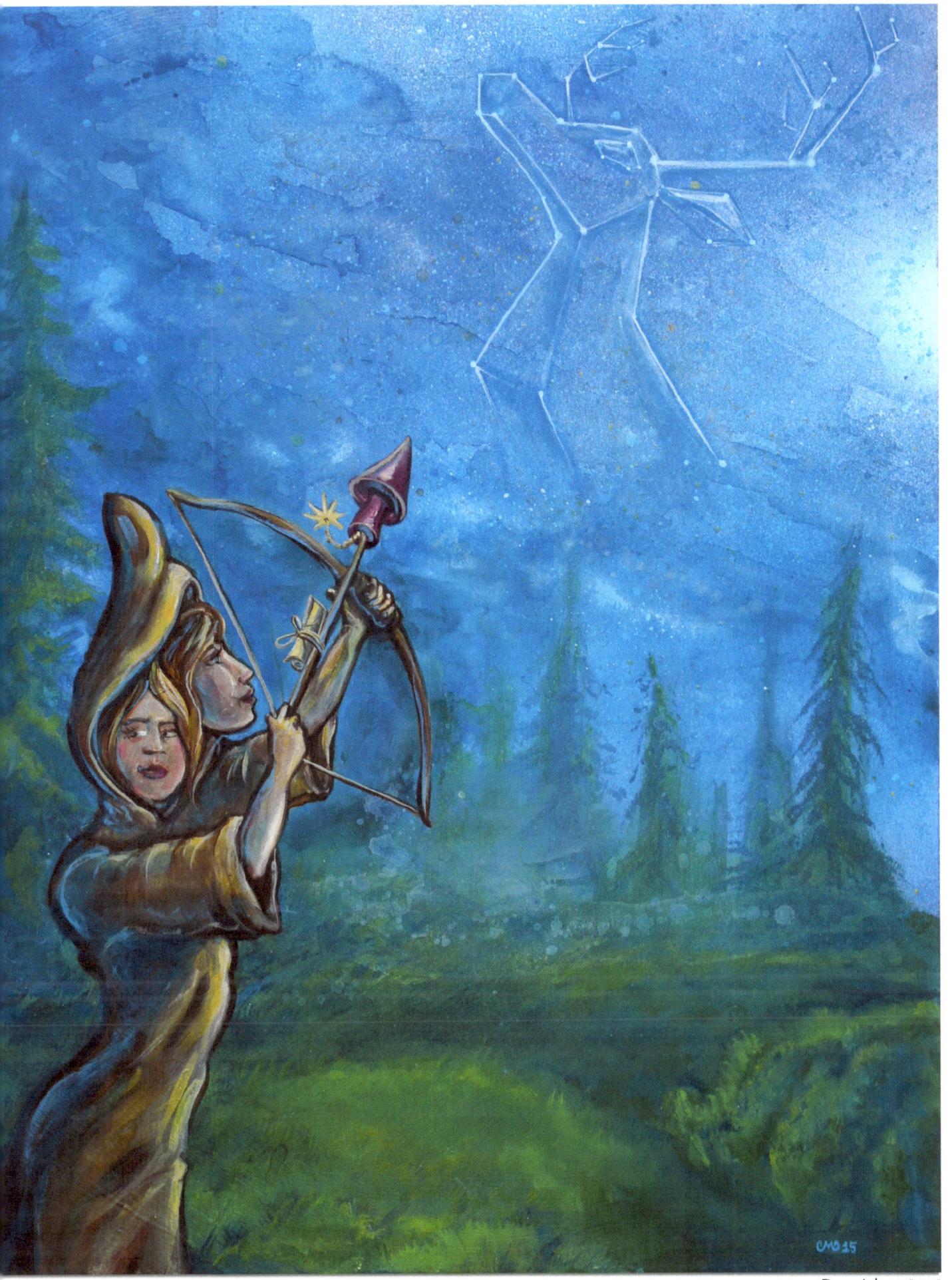

Deer John 18"x24"

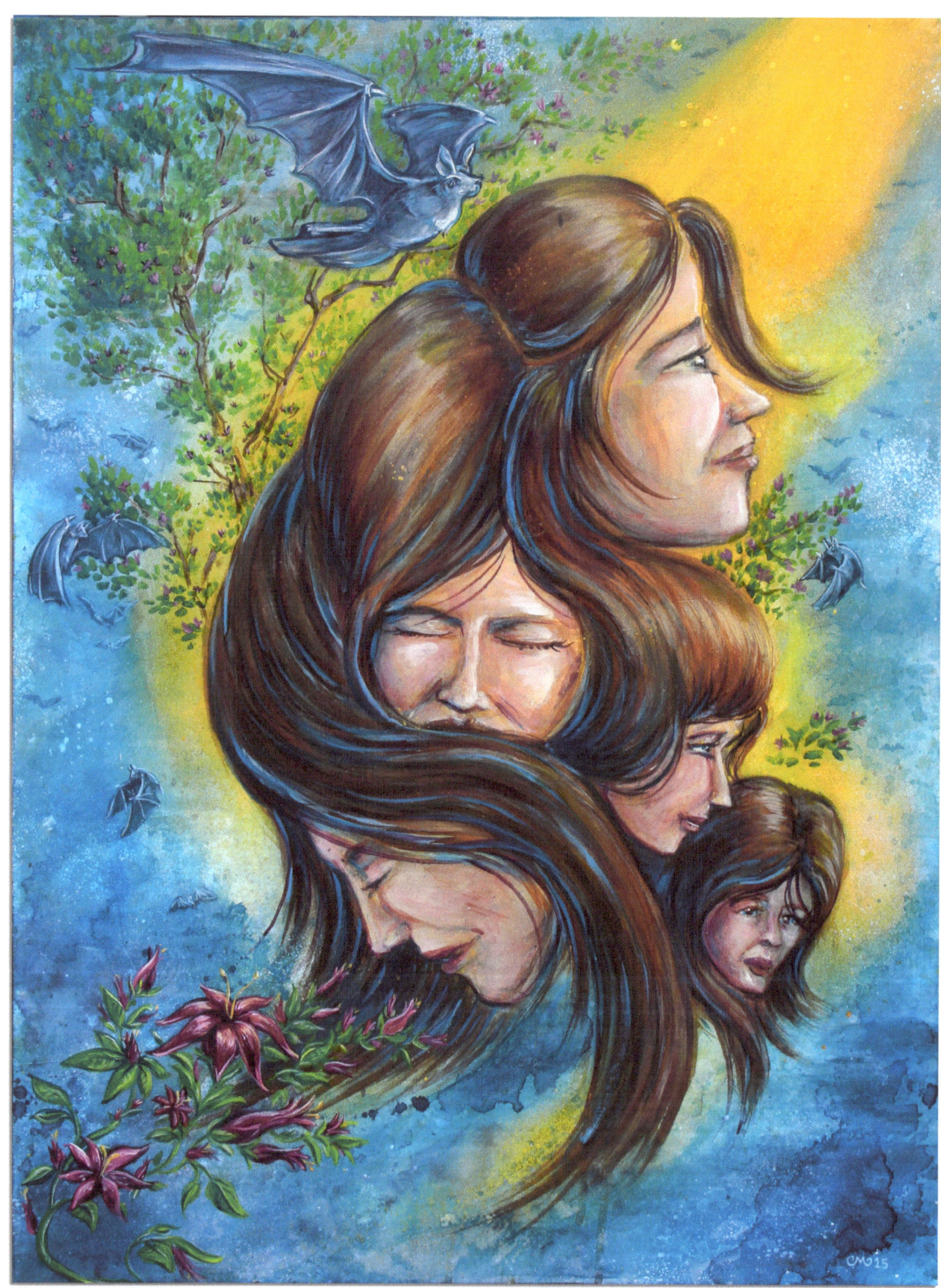

The Coming Light 18"x24"

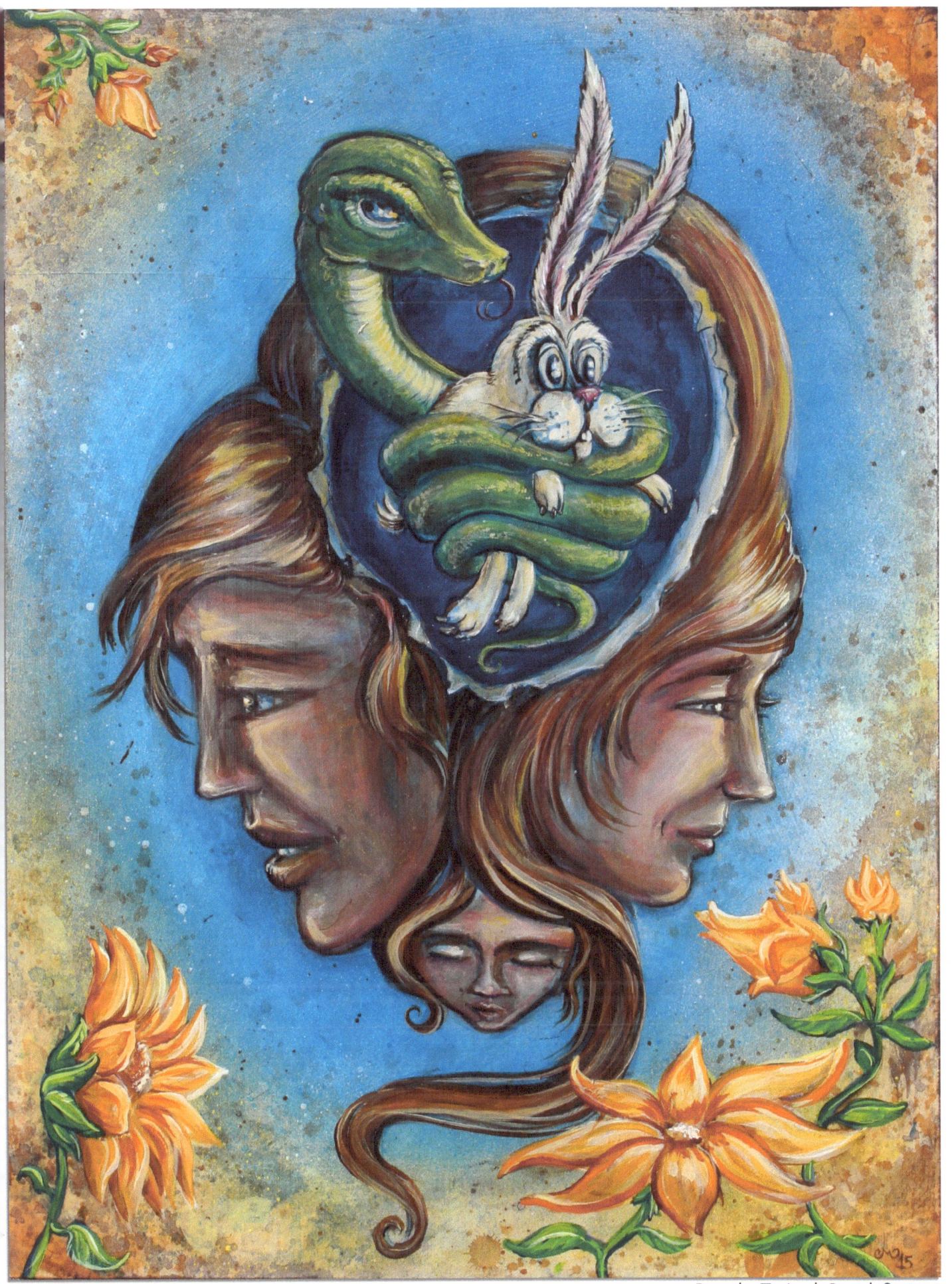

Does this Tie Look Straight? 18"x24"

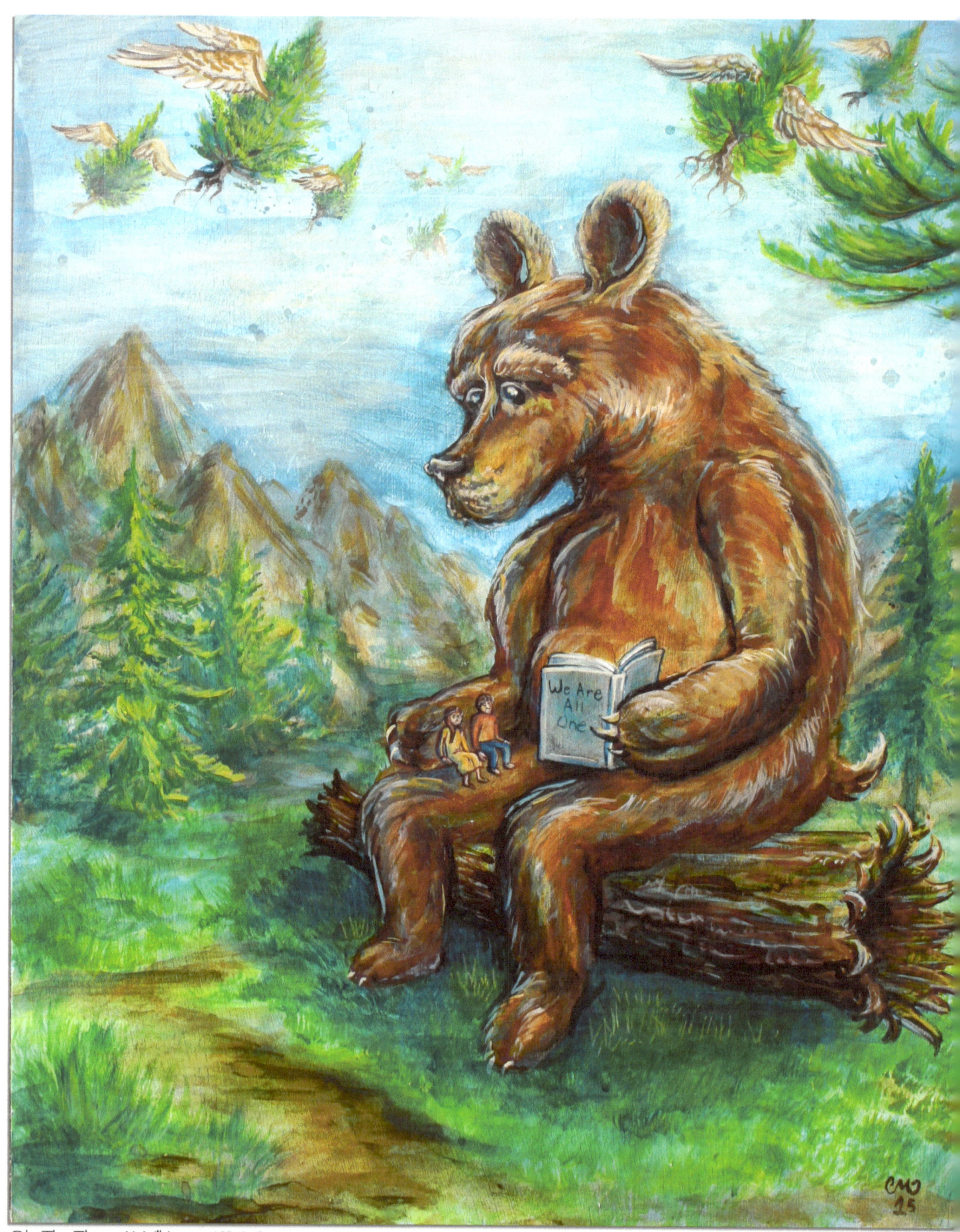

Oh, The Things We'll Learn 18"x24"

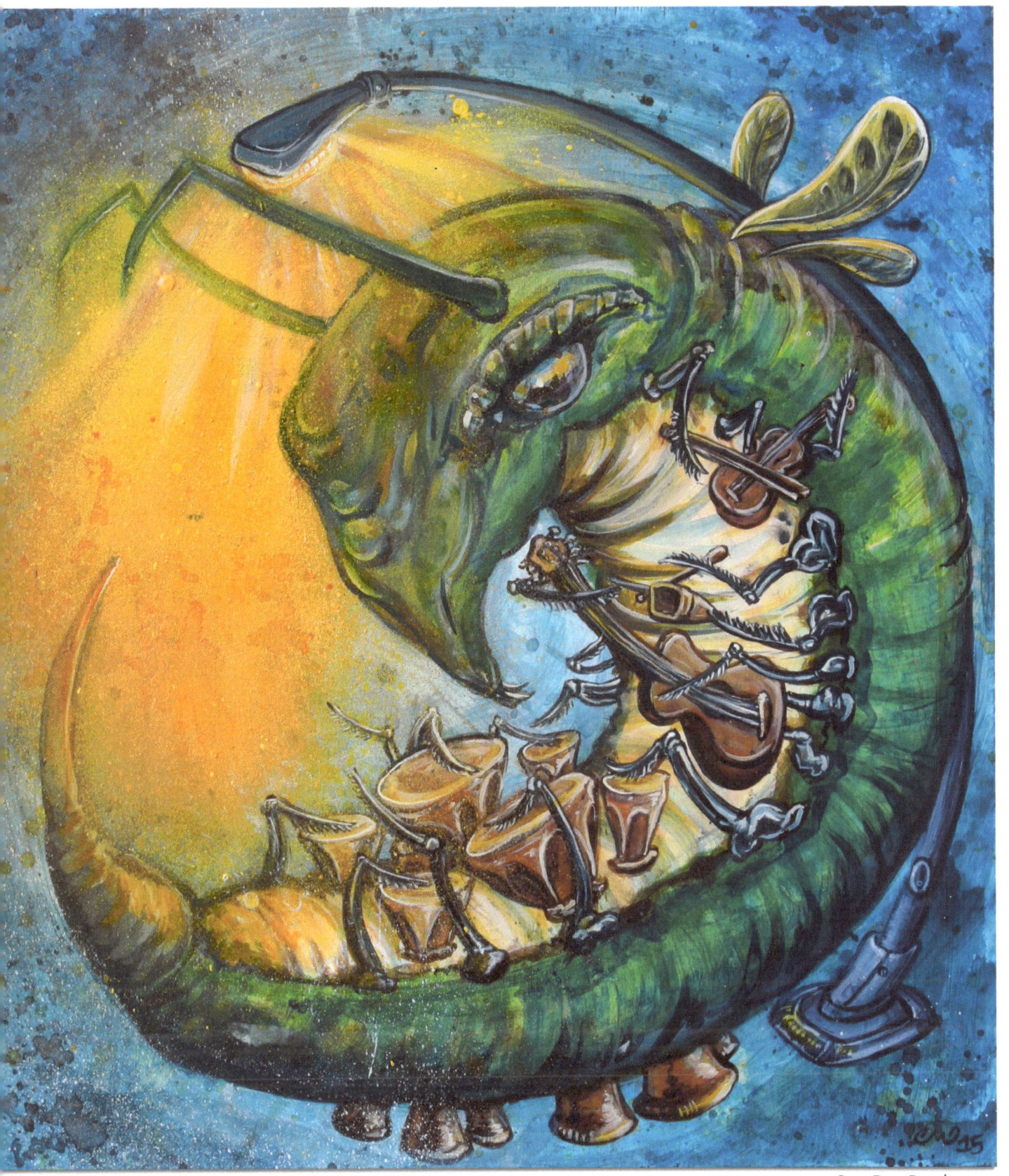

One Bug Band 14"x16"

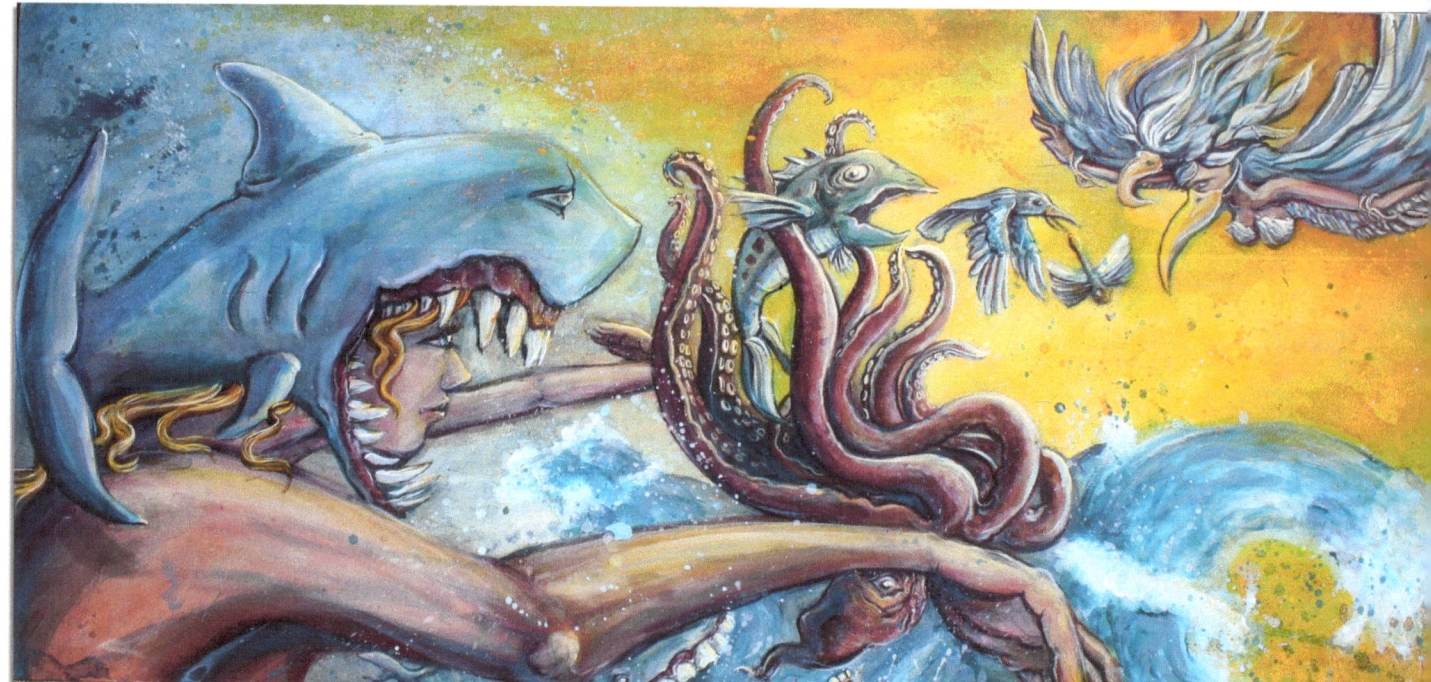

Usurper 48"x24"

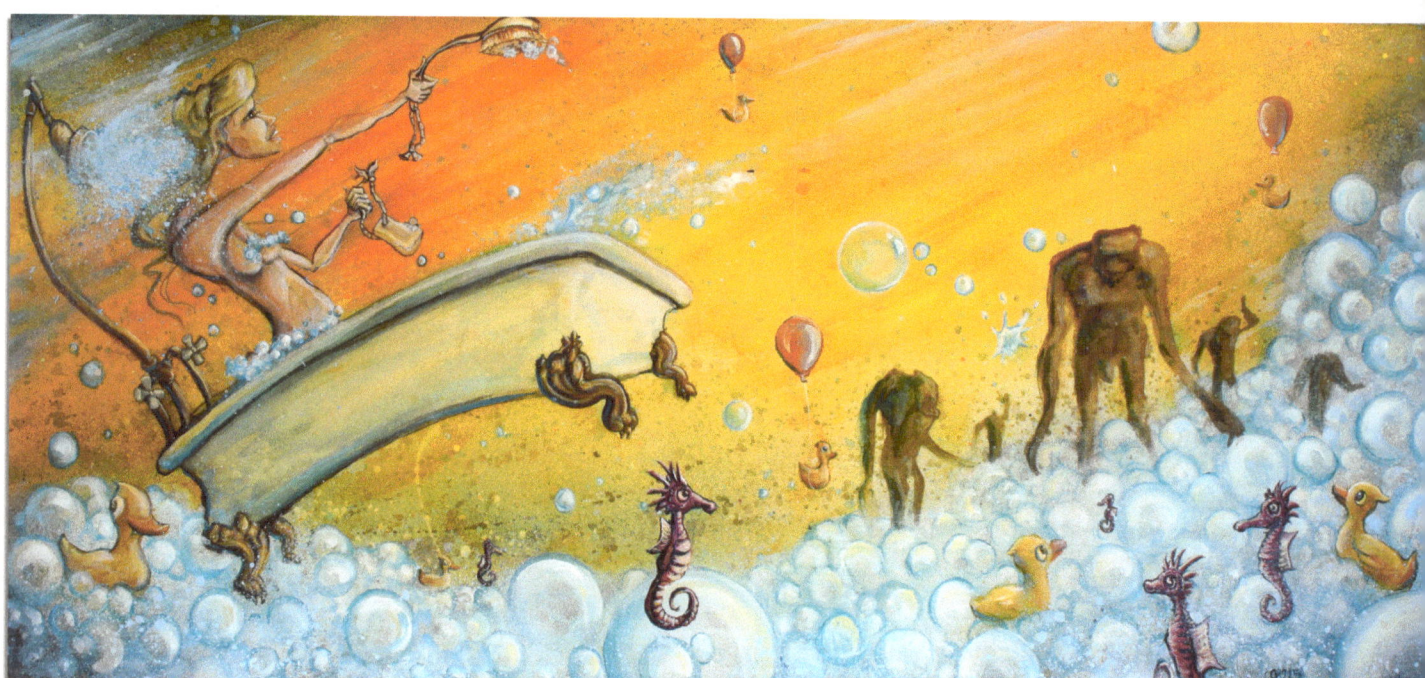

Clean Fight 48"x24"

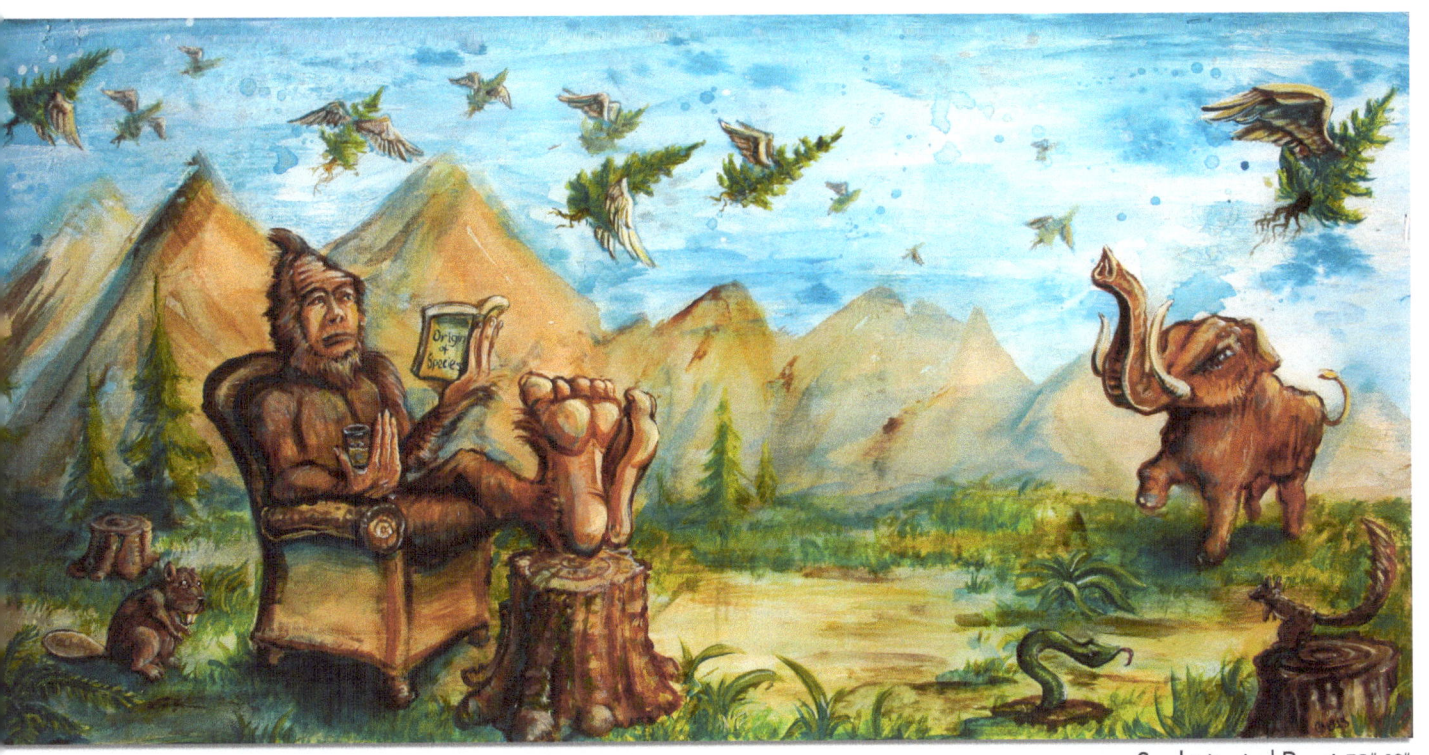

Sophisticated Beast 32"x18"

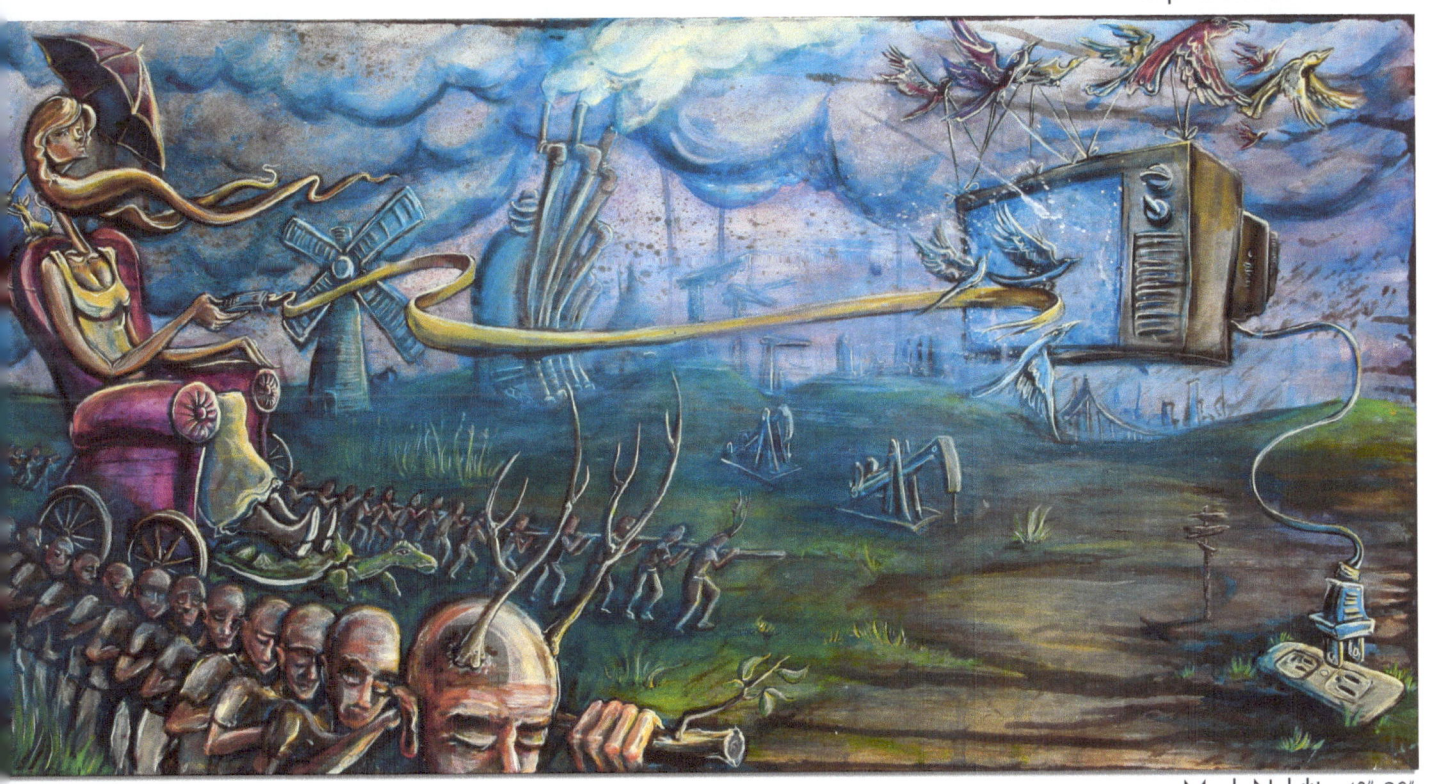

Meek Nobility 48"x28"

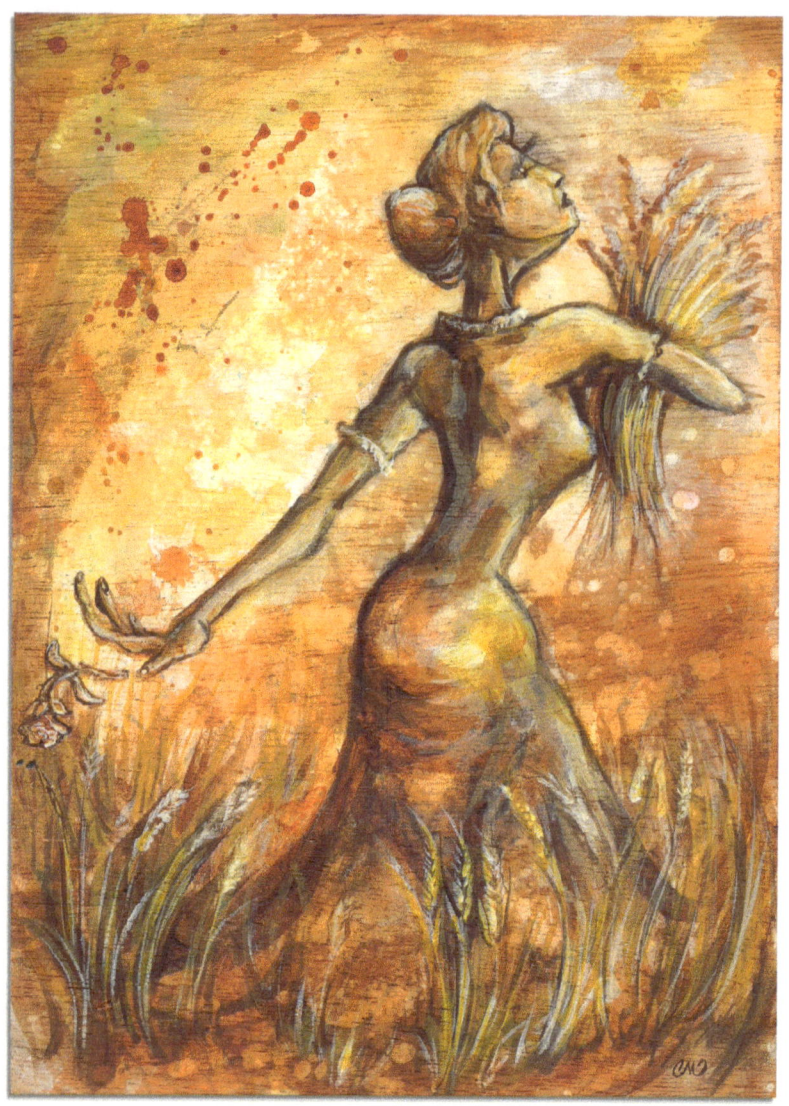

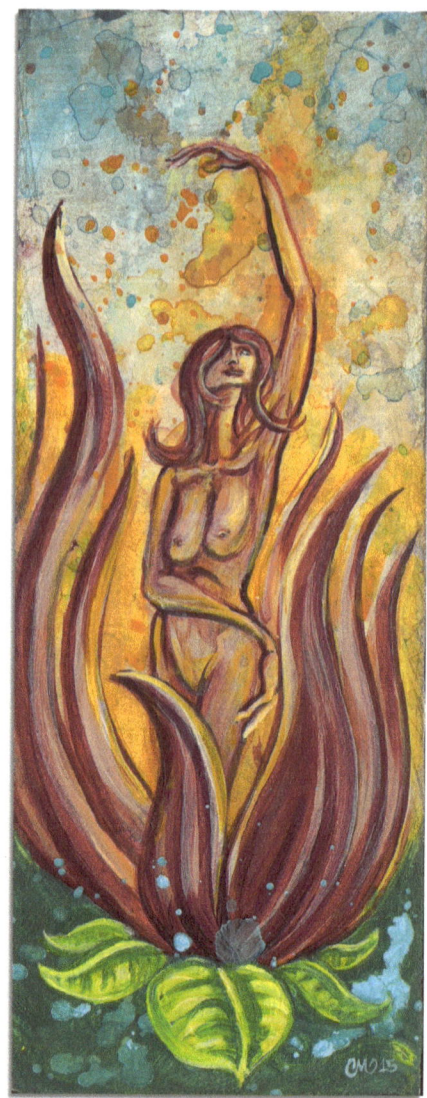

Wheat from the Chaff 6"x9"

Flowering Inferno 2"x6"

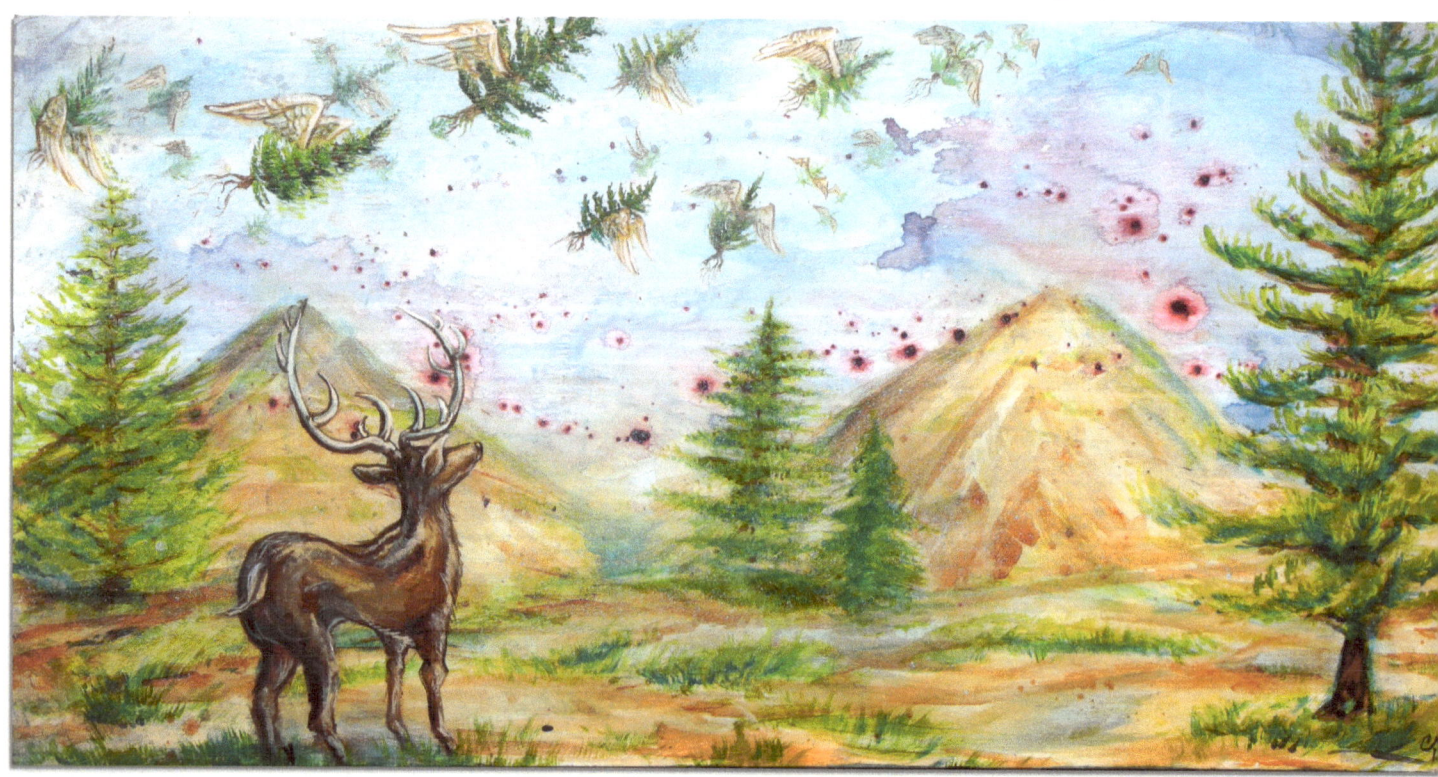

Observer 12"x24"

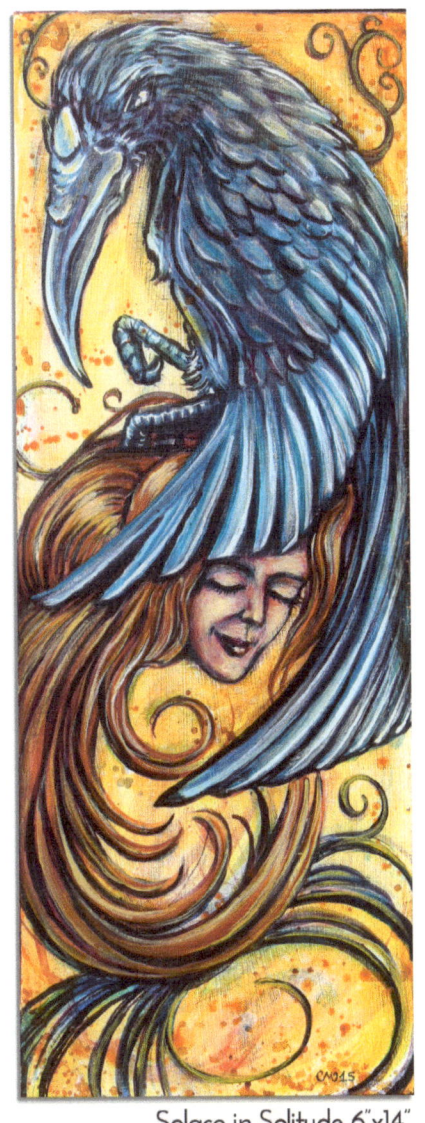

Solace in Solitude 6"x14"

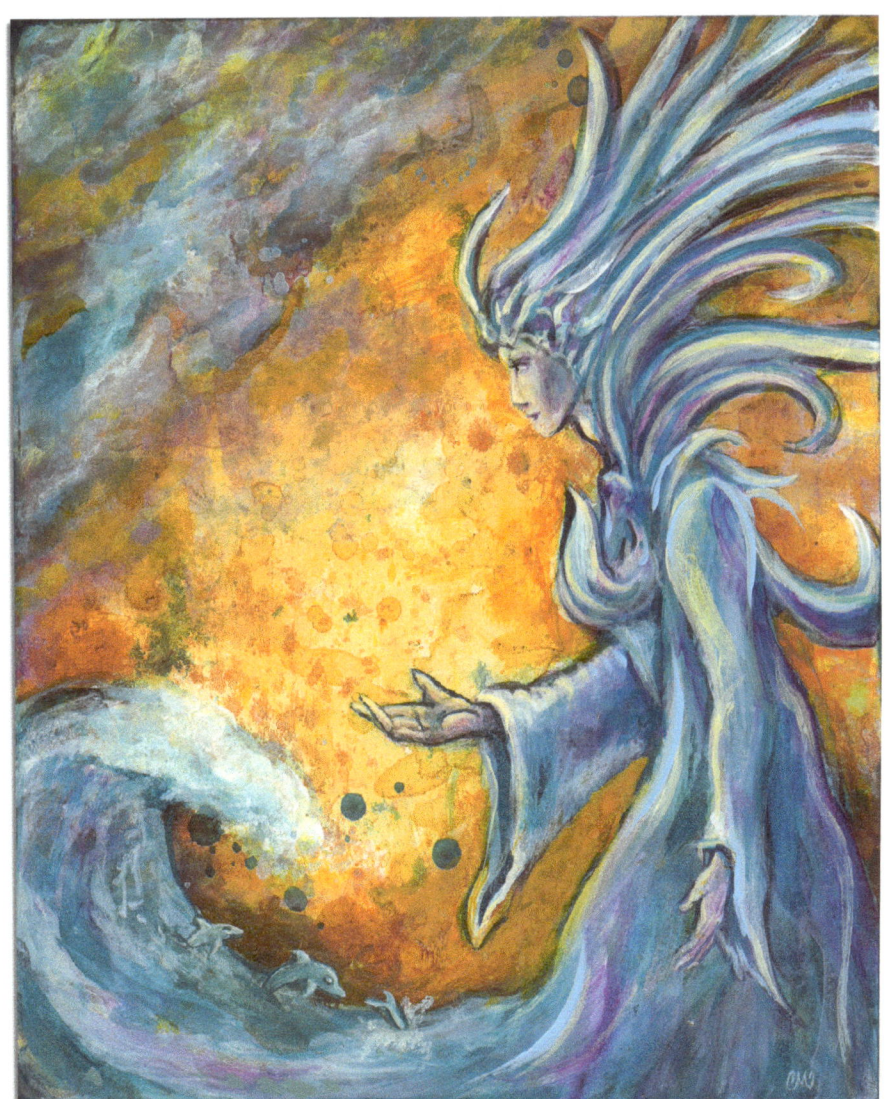

Guiding Hand 6"x12"

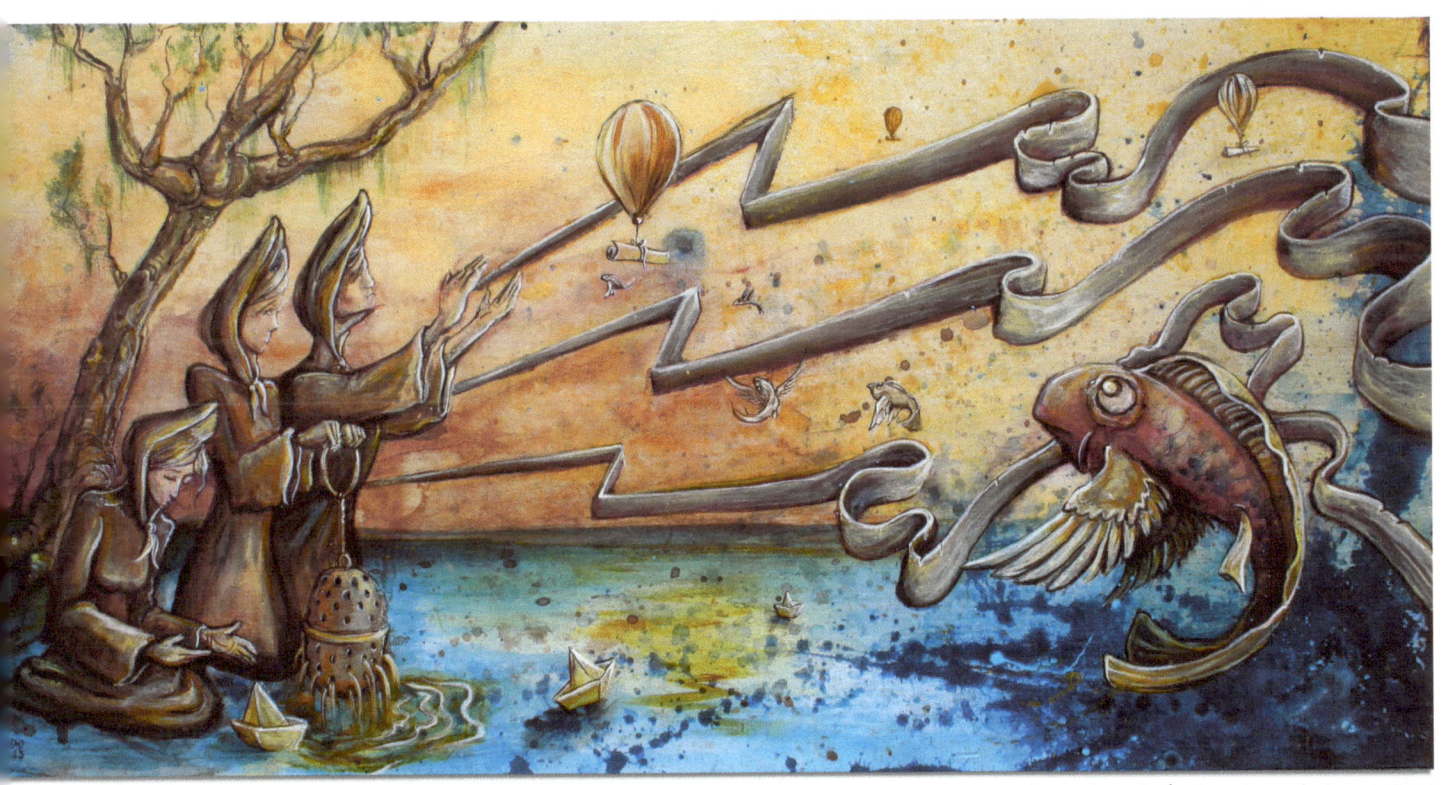

Aspiration, Indoctrination, Action 24"x12"

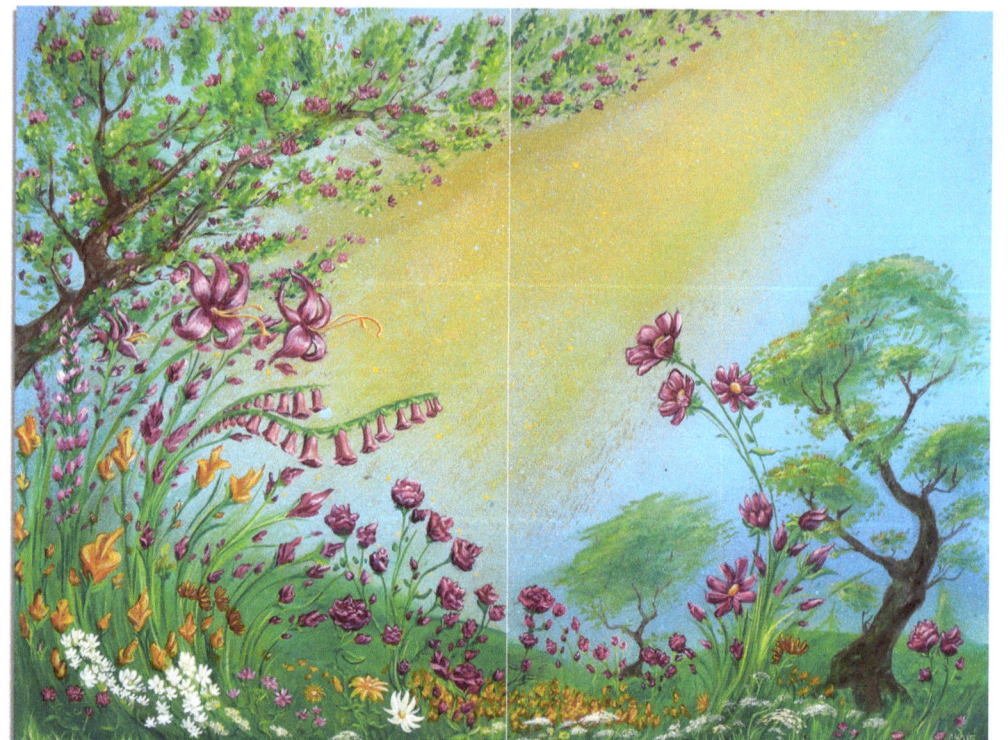

Flowers in Motion (2) 18"x24"

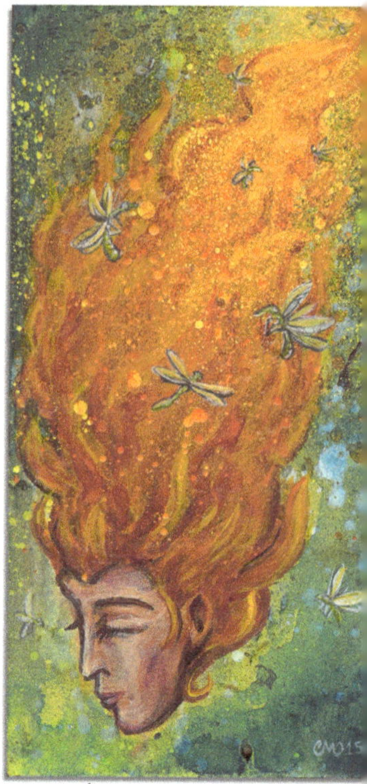

Inspired Fire 6"x12"

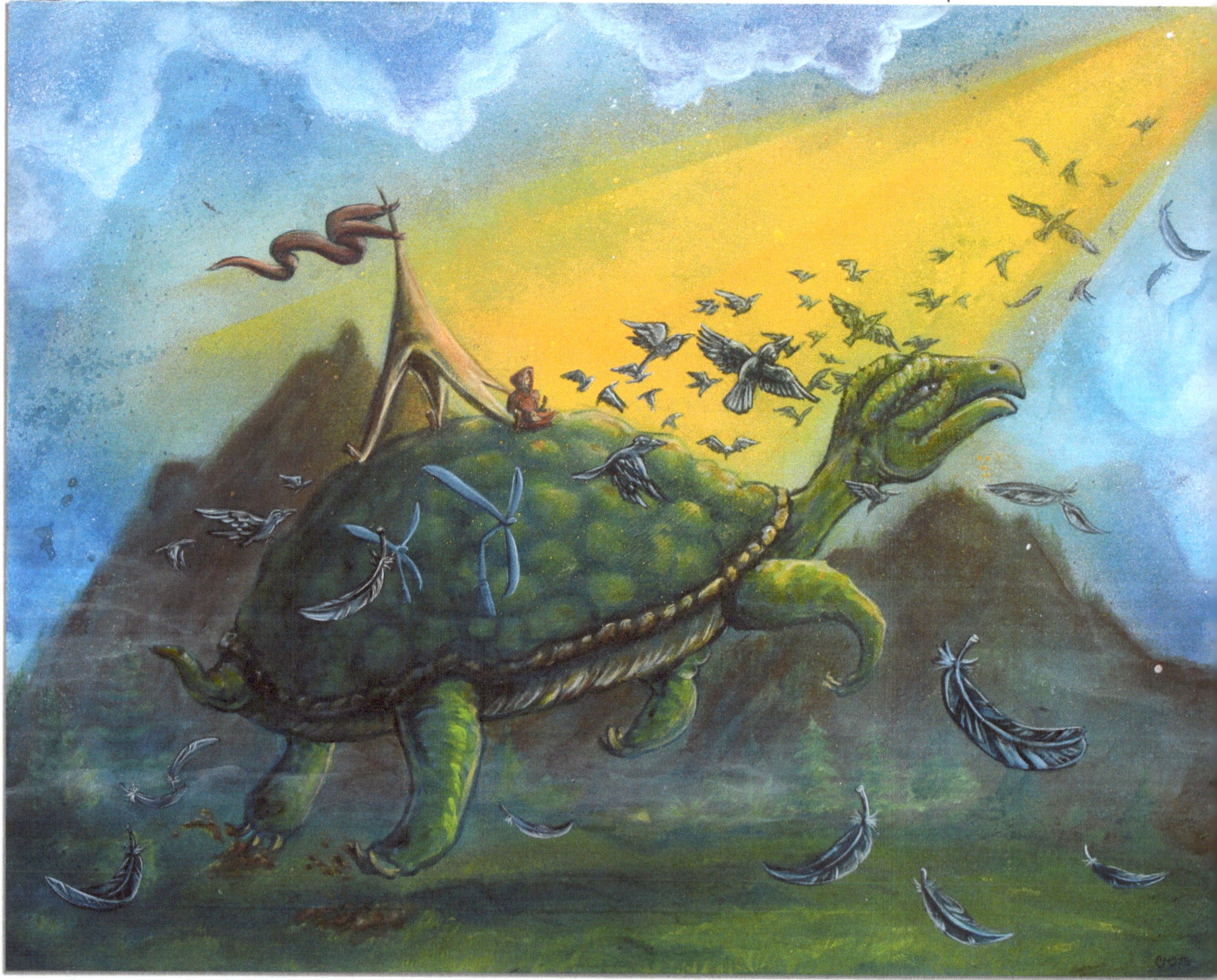

Ascend (We Can Do This!) 30"x24"

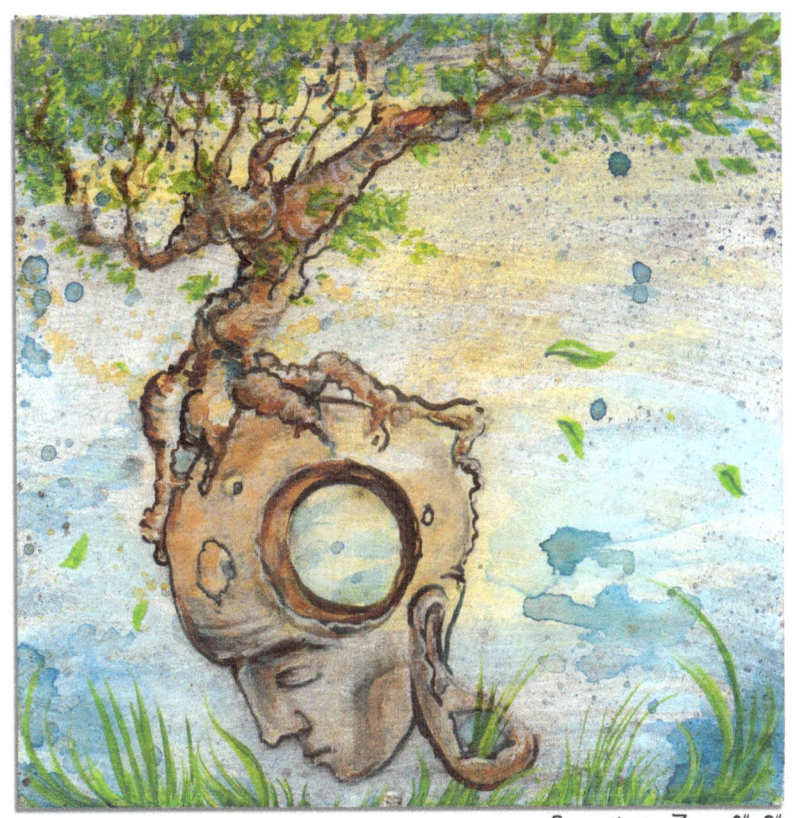

Serenity in Zero 8"x8"

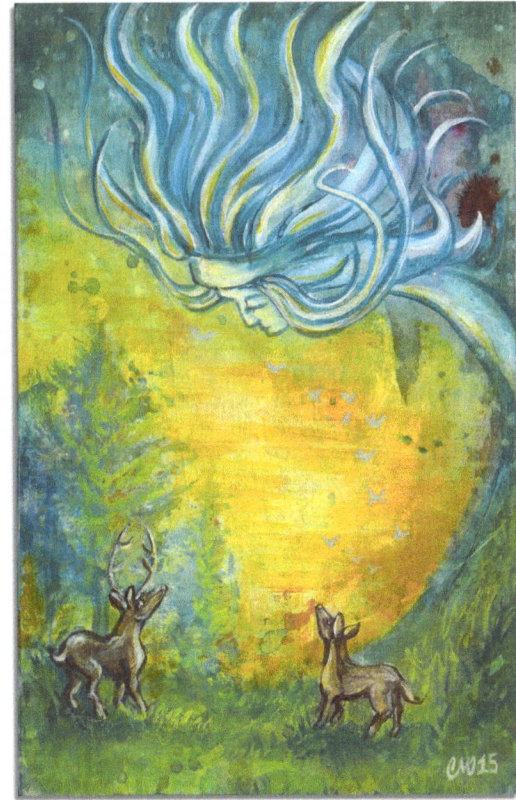

Mother Night 6"x9"

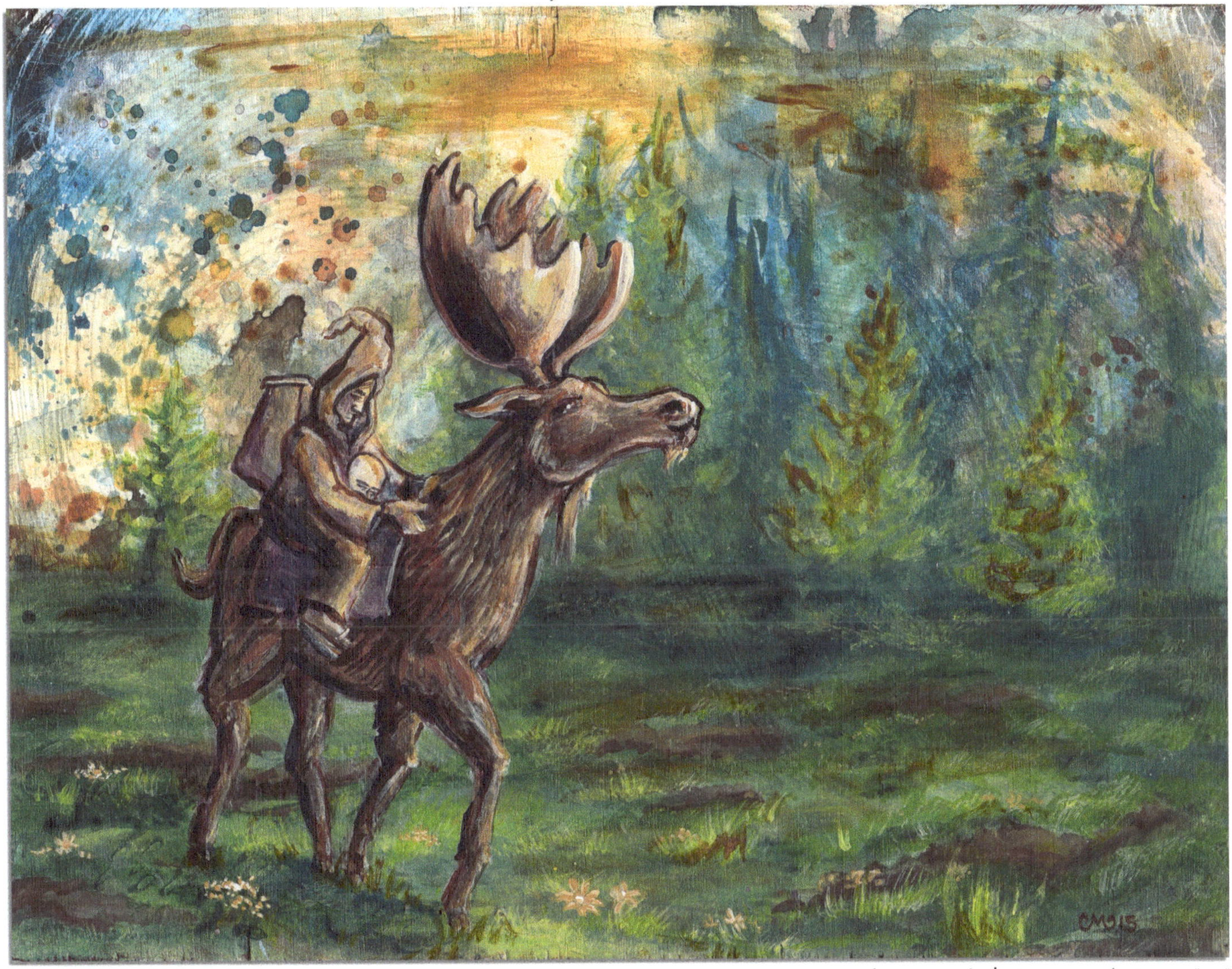

Aspiration, Indoctrination, Action 24"x12"

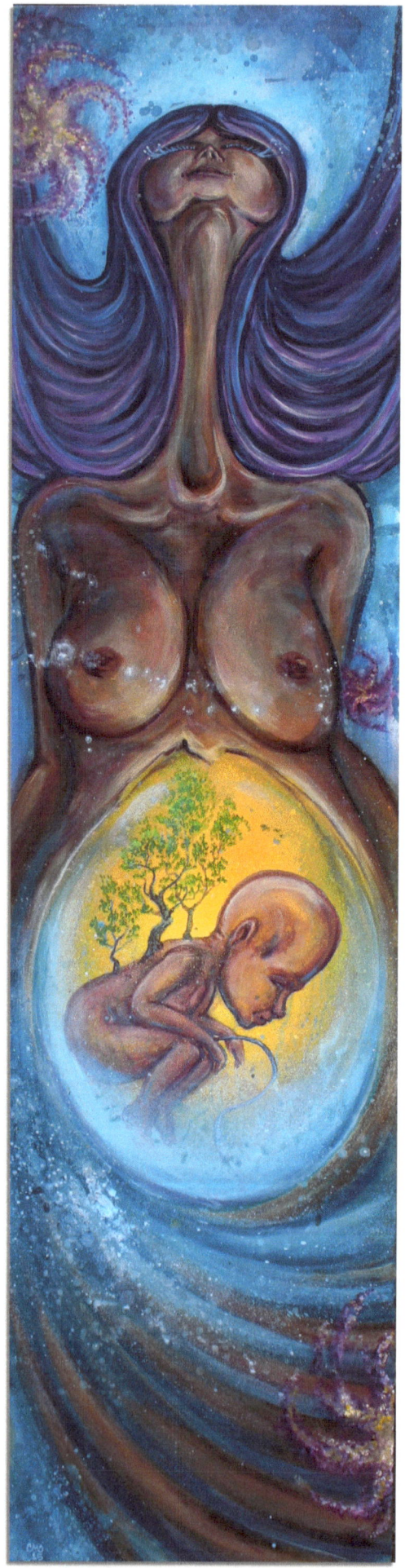

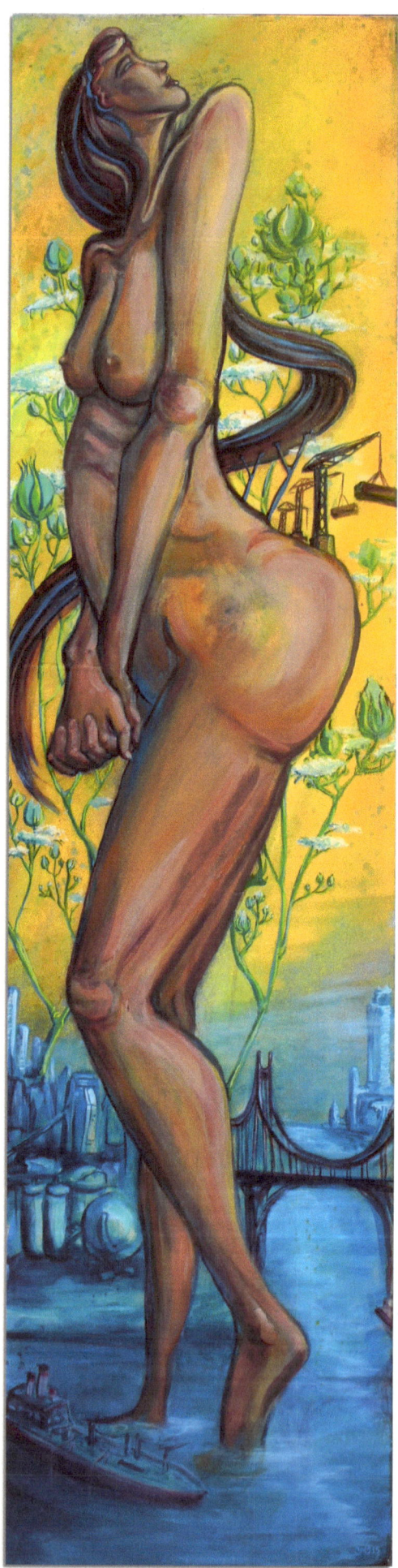

Teach Your Children Well 12"x48"   Aspiring to Build Better Bridges 12"x48"

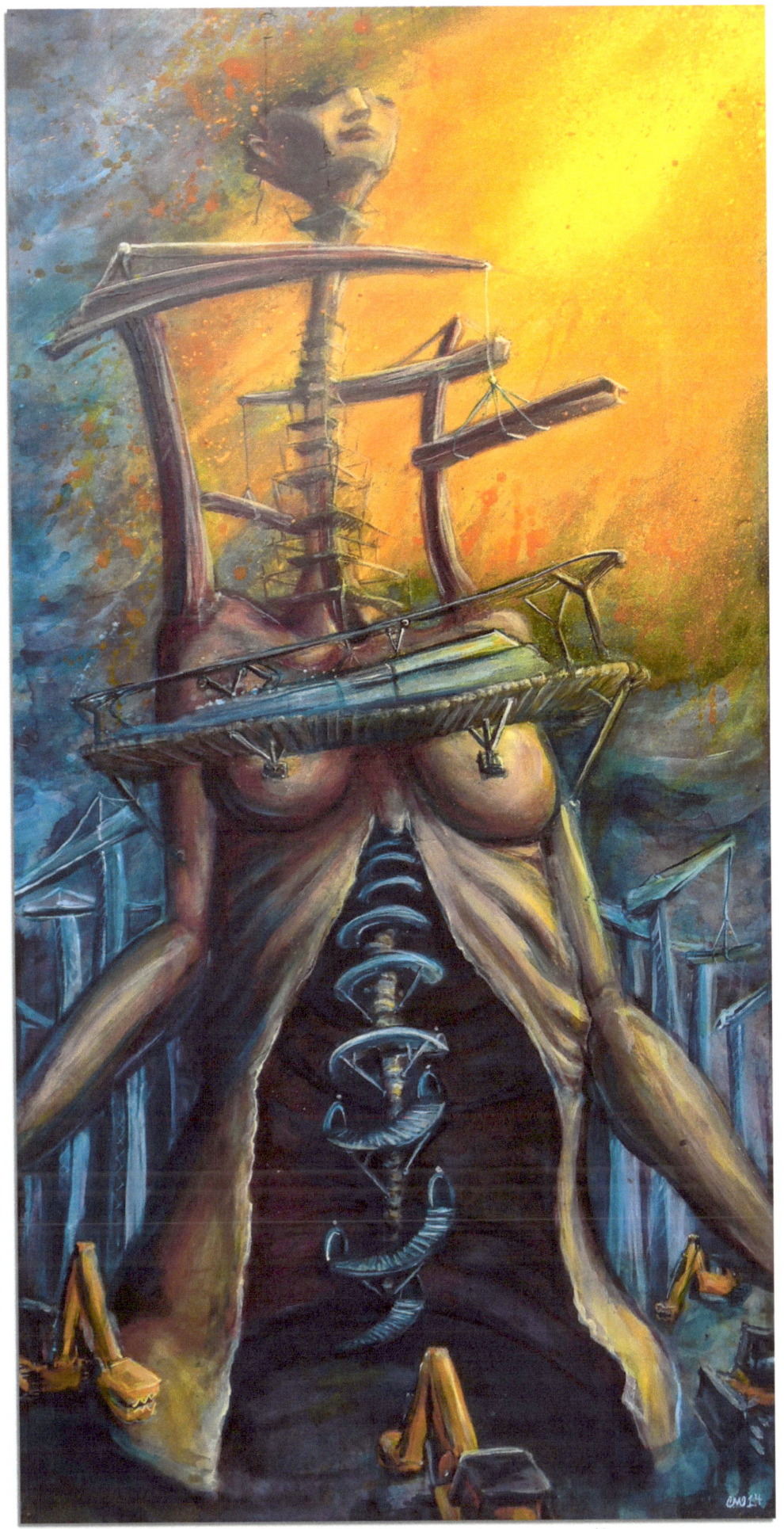

Self Construction 24"x48"

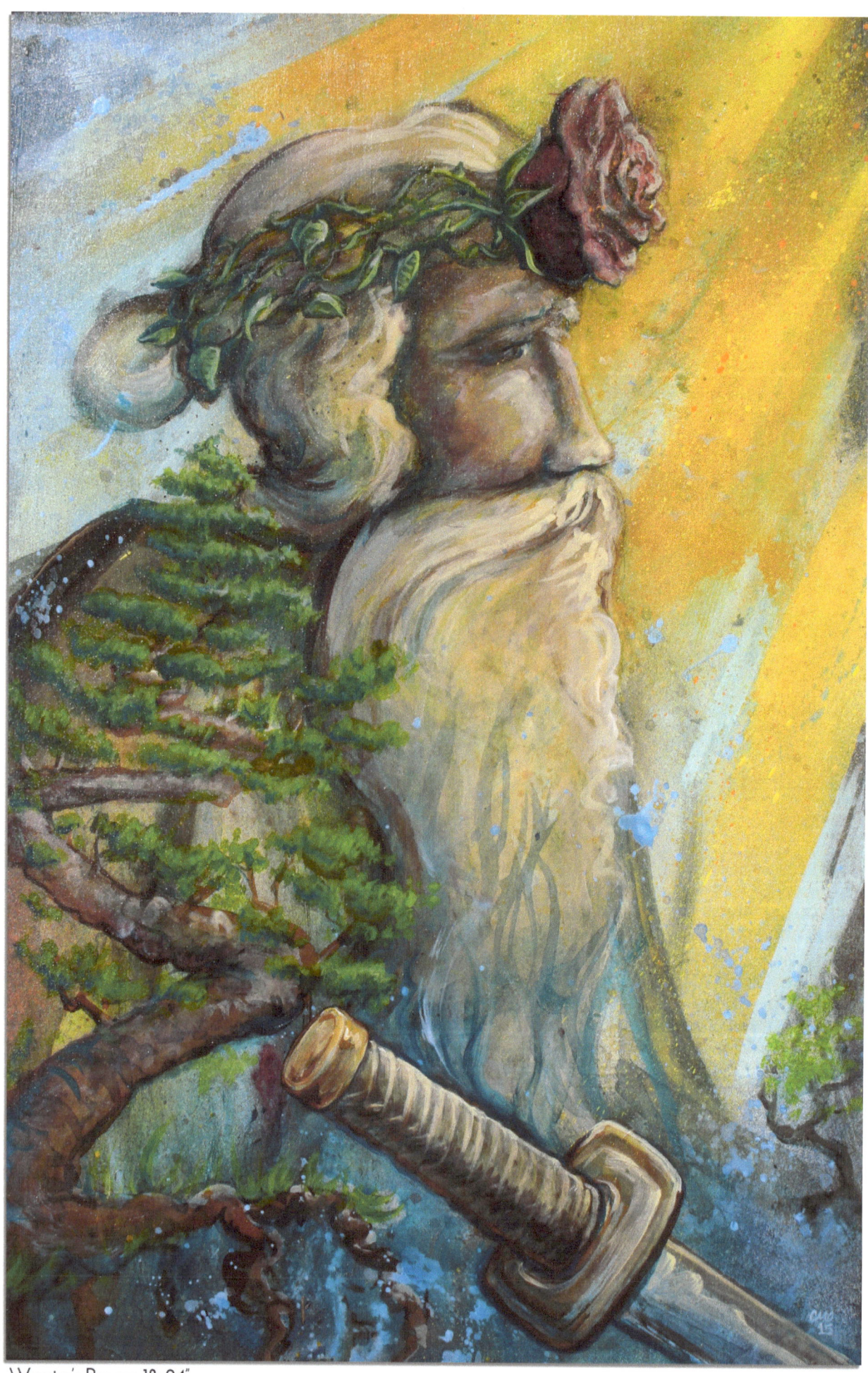

Warrior's Repose 18x24"

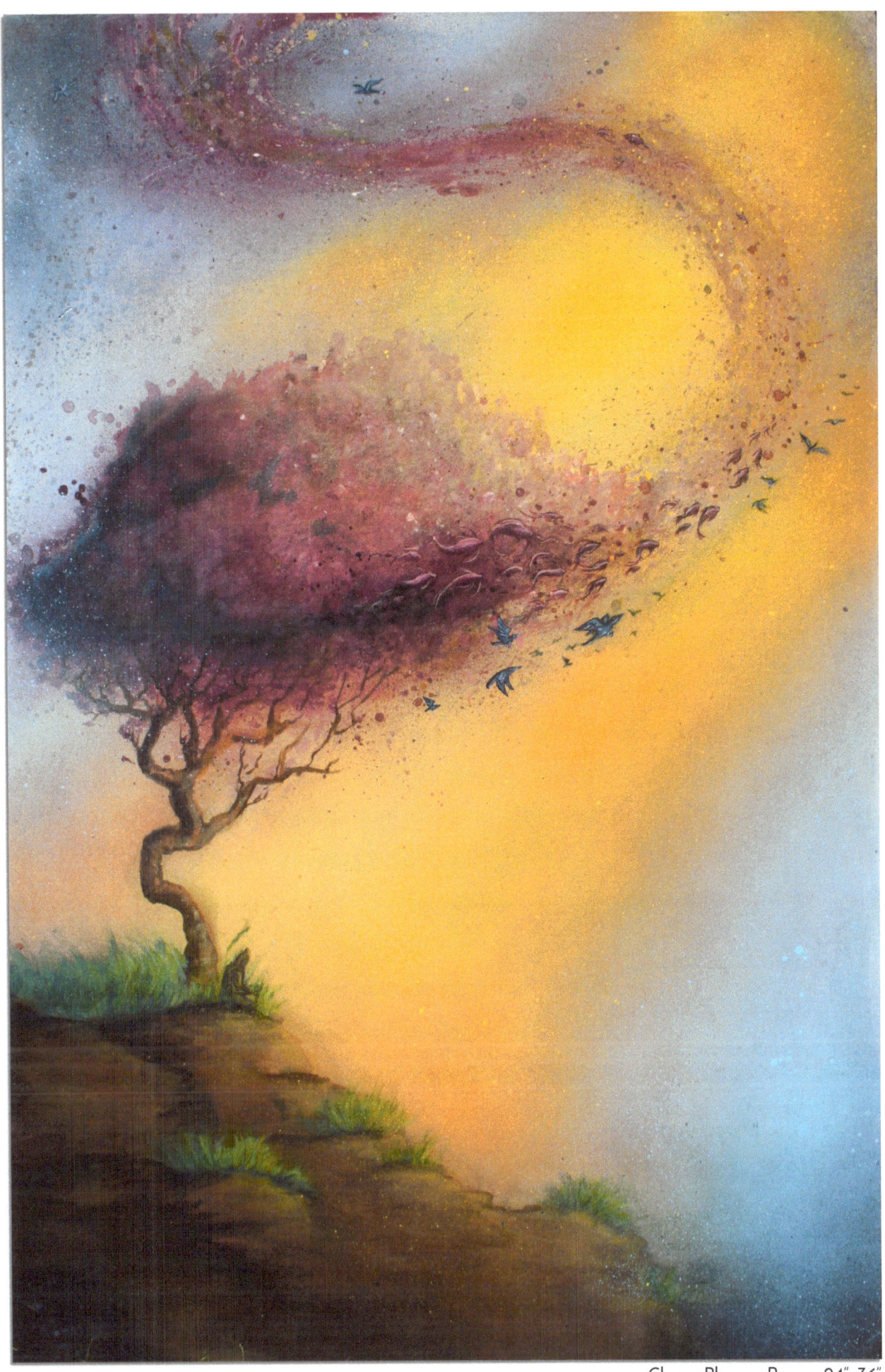

Cherry Blossom Breeze 24"x36"

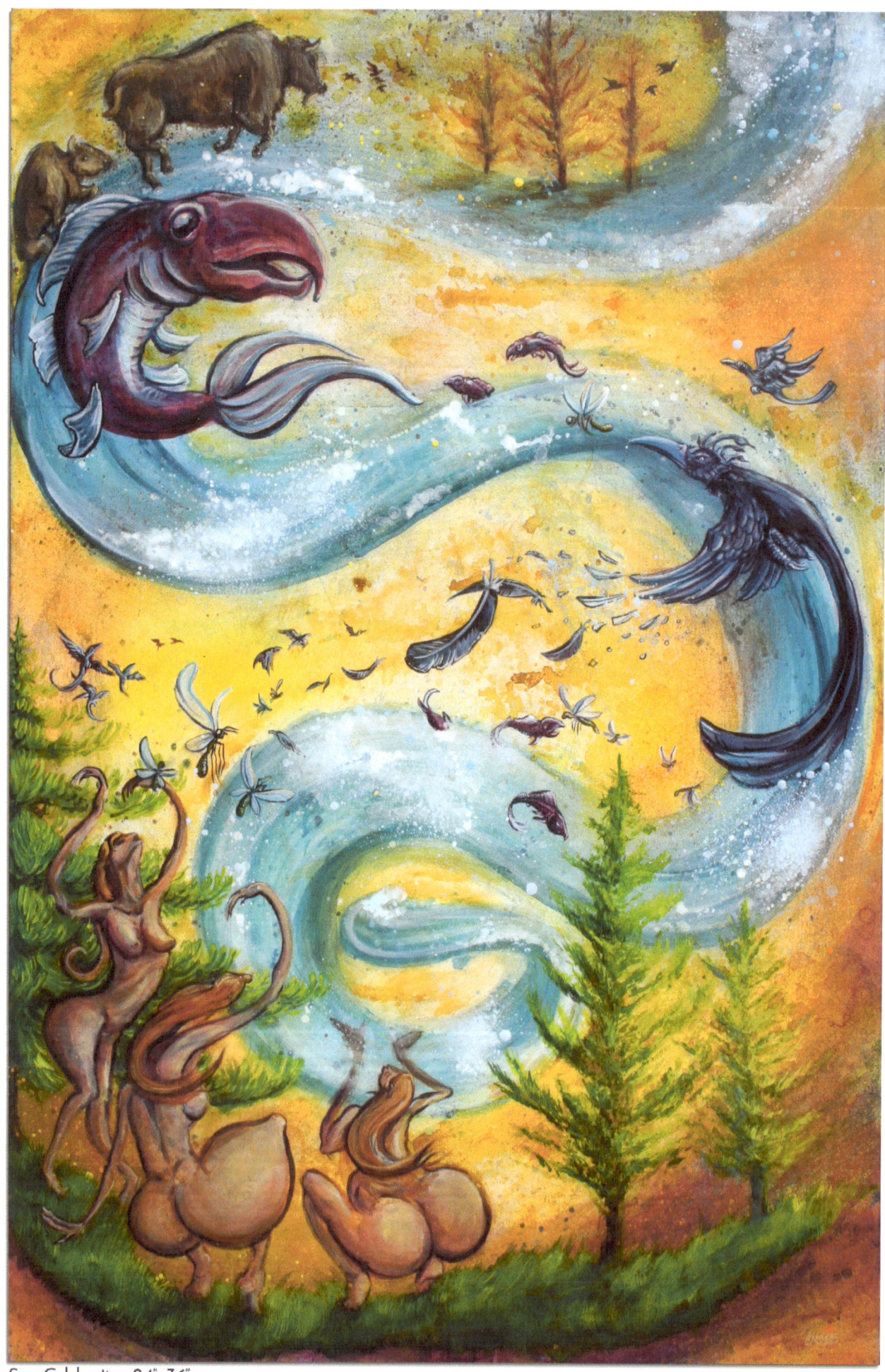

Sun Celebration 24"x36"

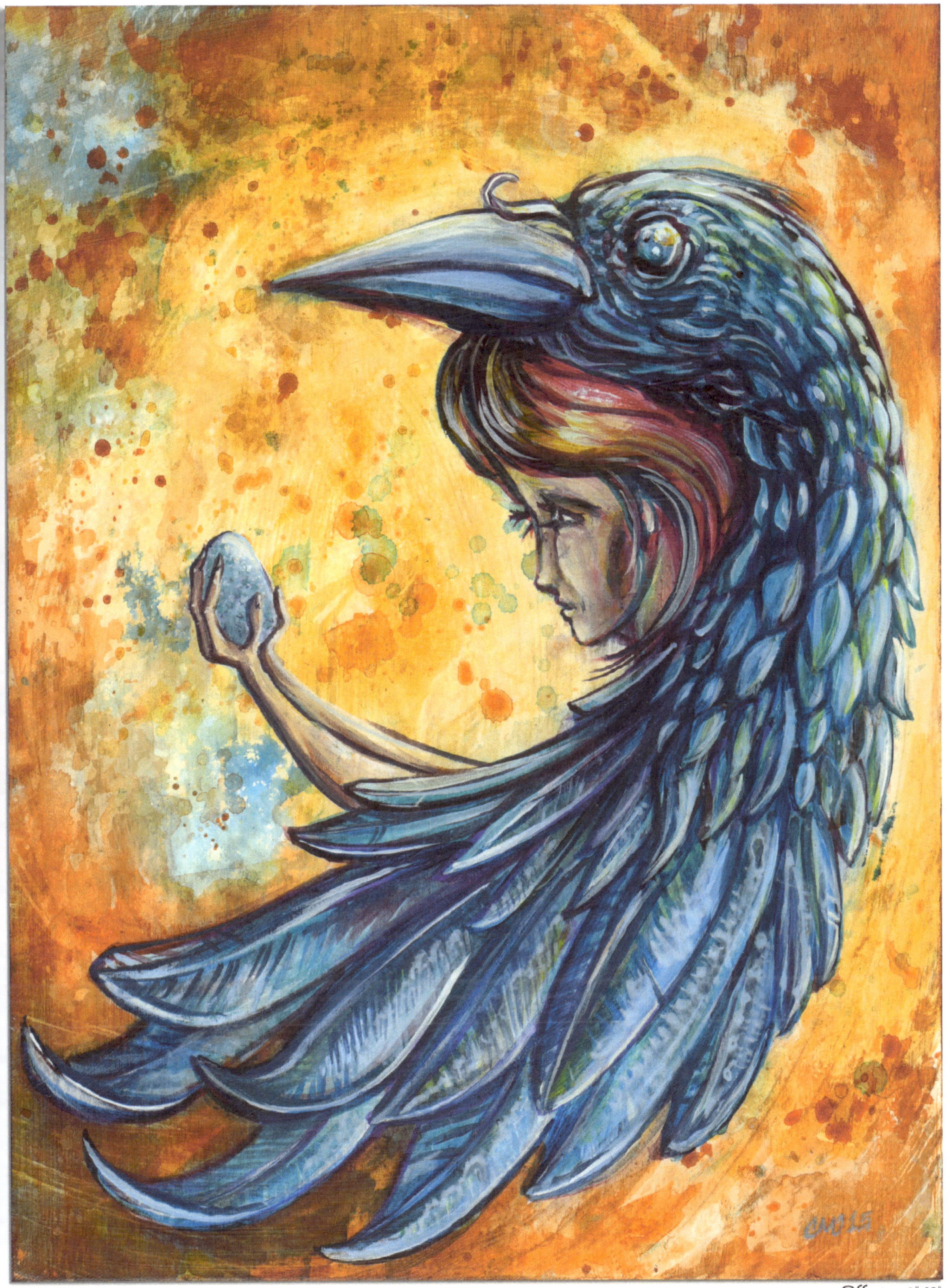

Offering 9"x12"

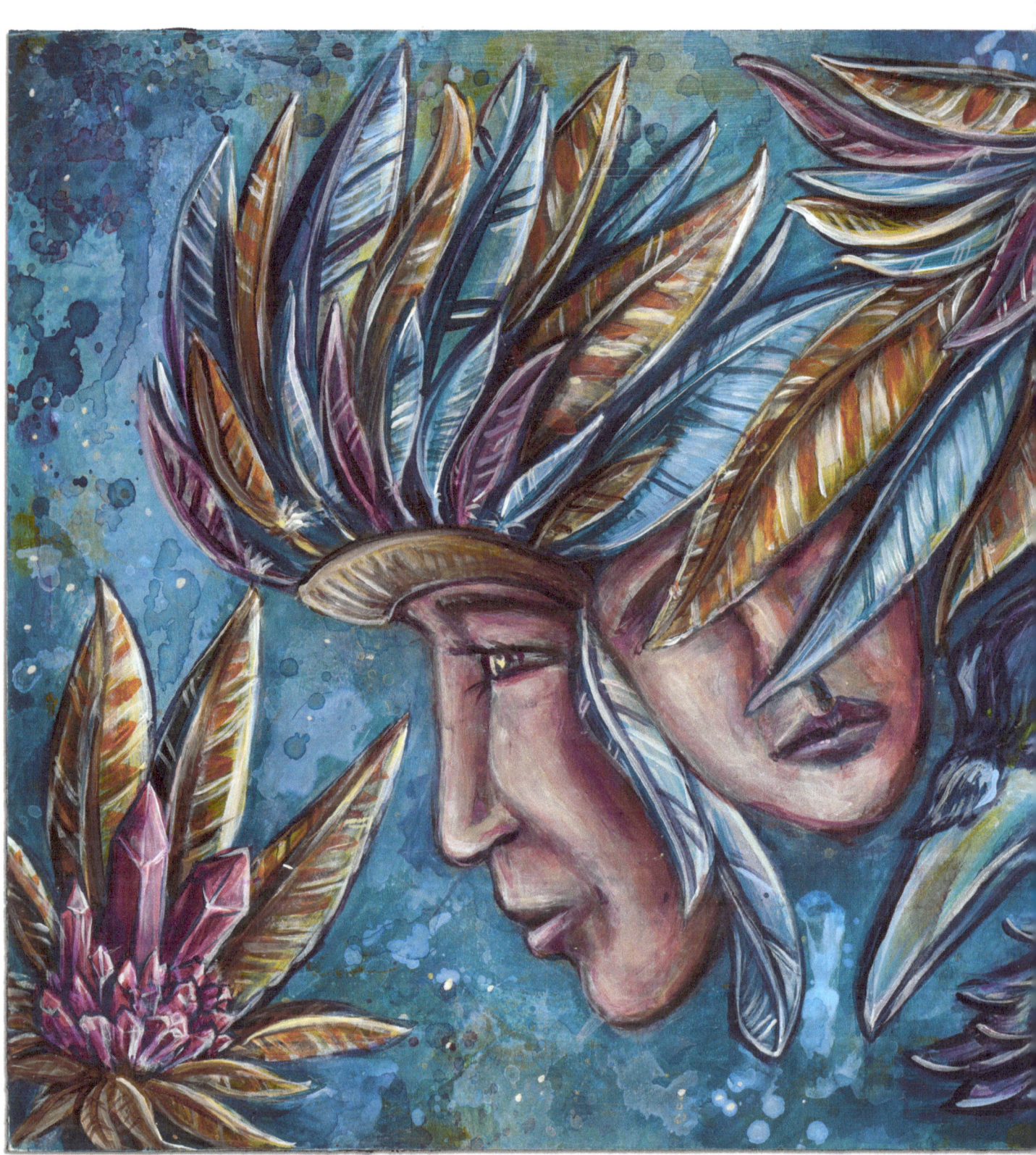

Better In Tune With The Infinite (2) 12"x12"

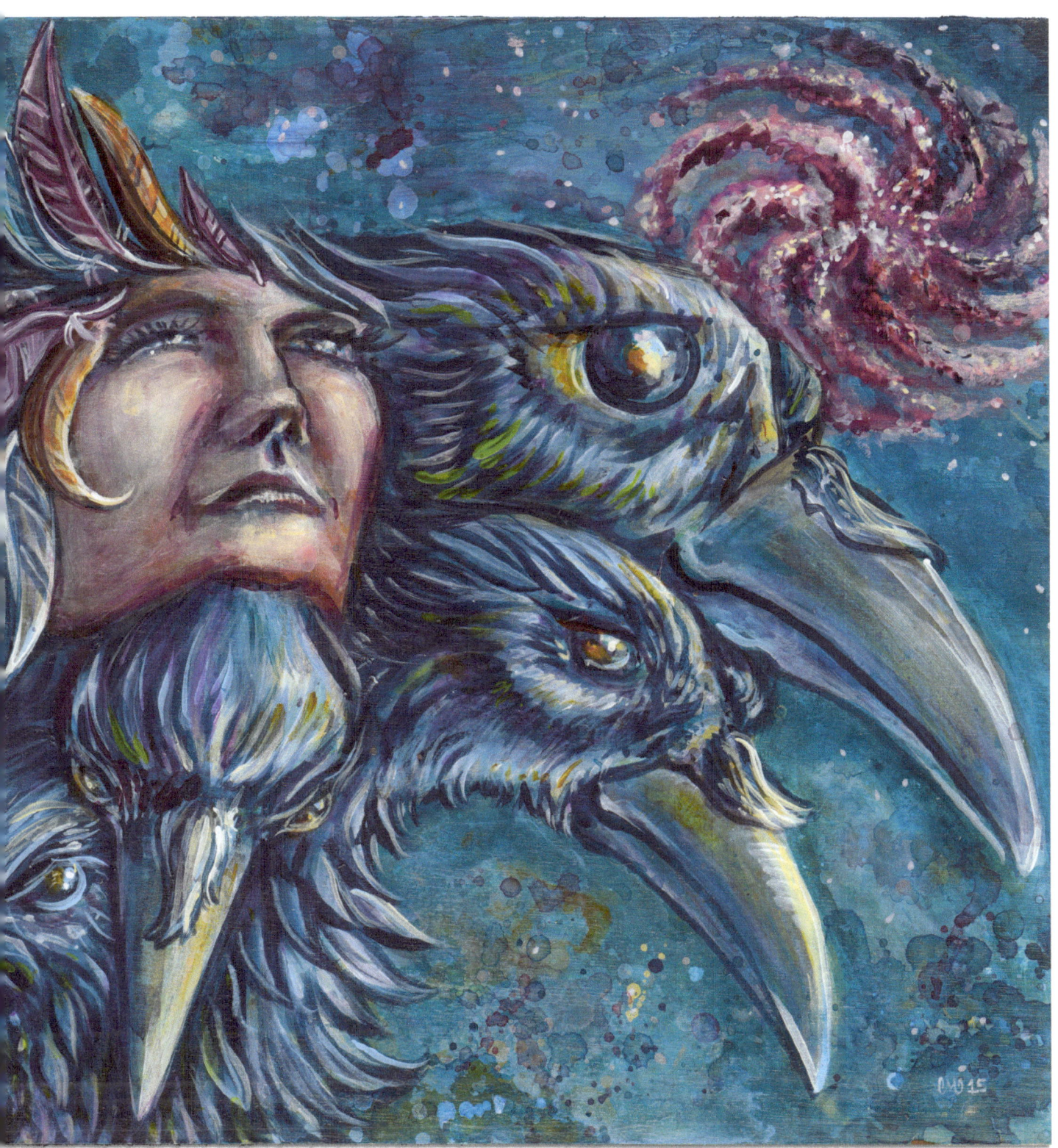

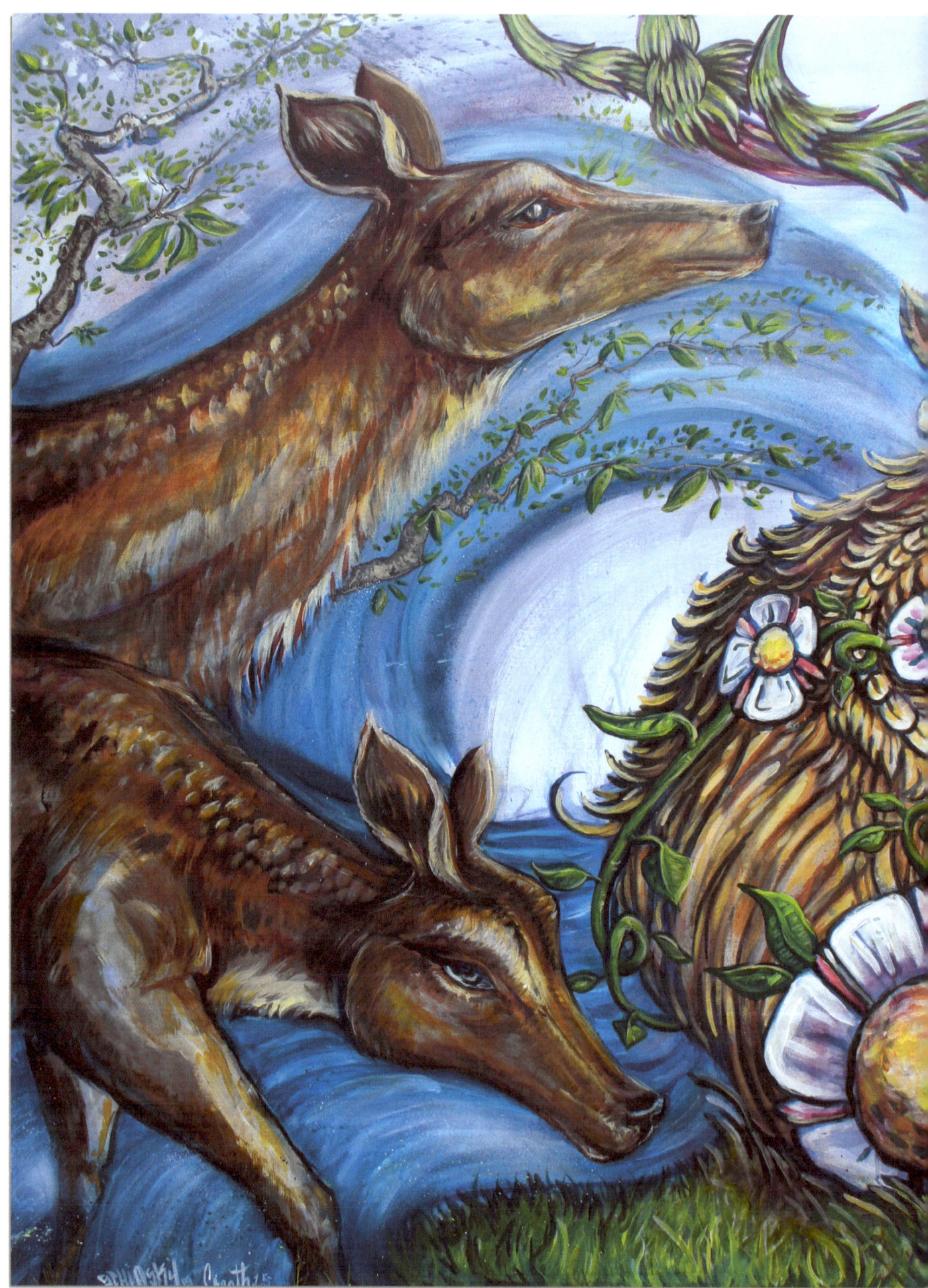

Tony Danza Collaboration with Matt Schlosky (2) 36"x48"

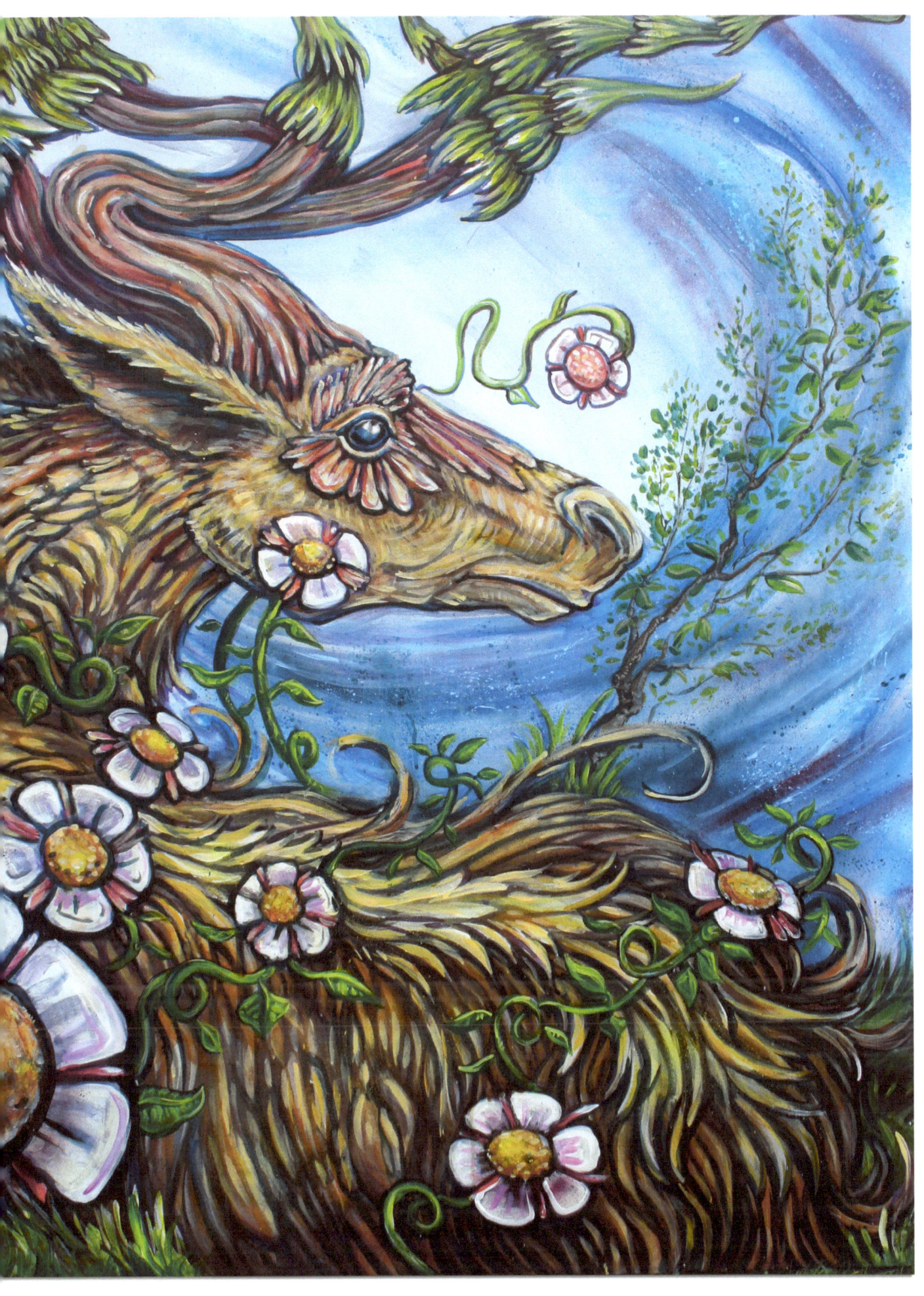

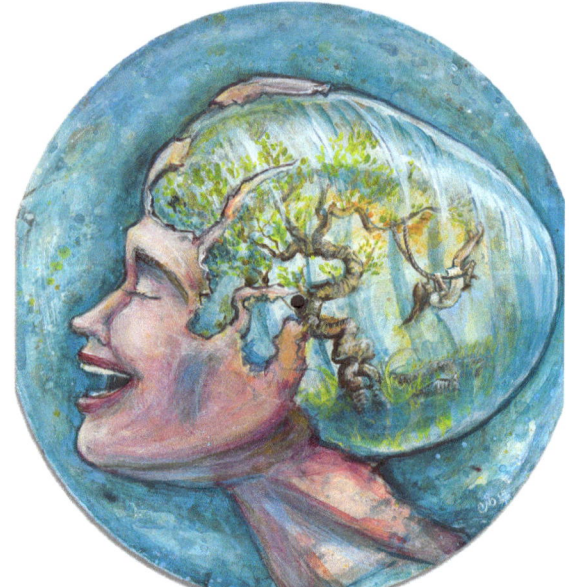

Reminisce 12" Vinyl Record

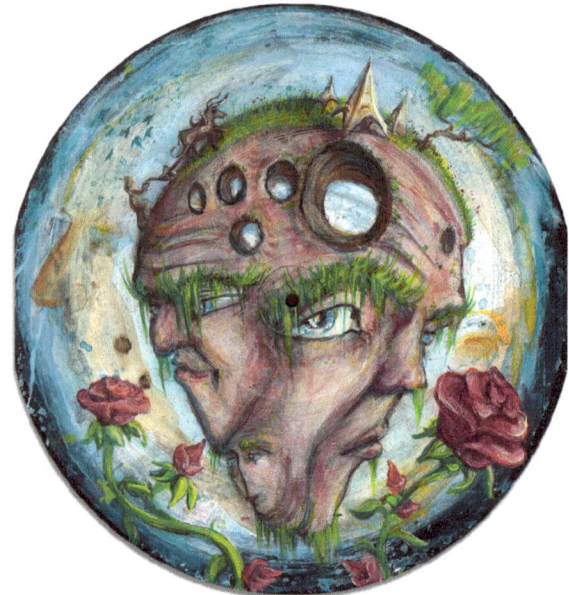

Reep & Sow 12" Vinyl Record

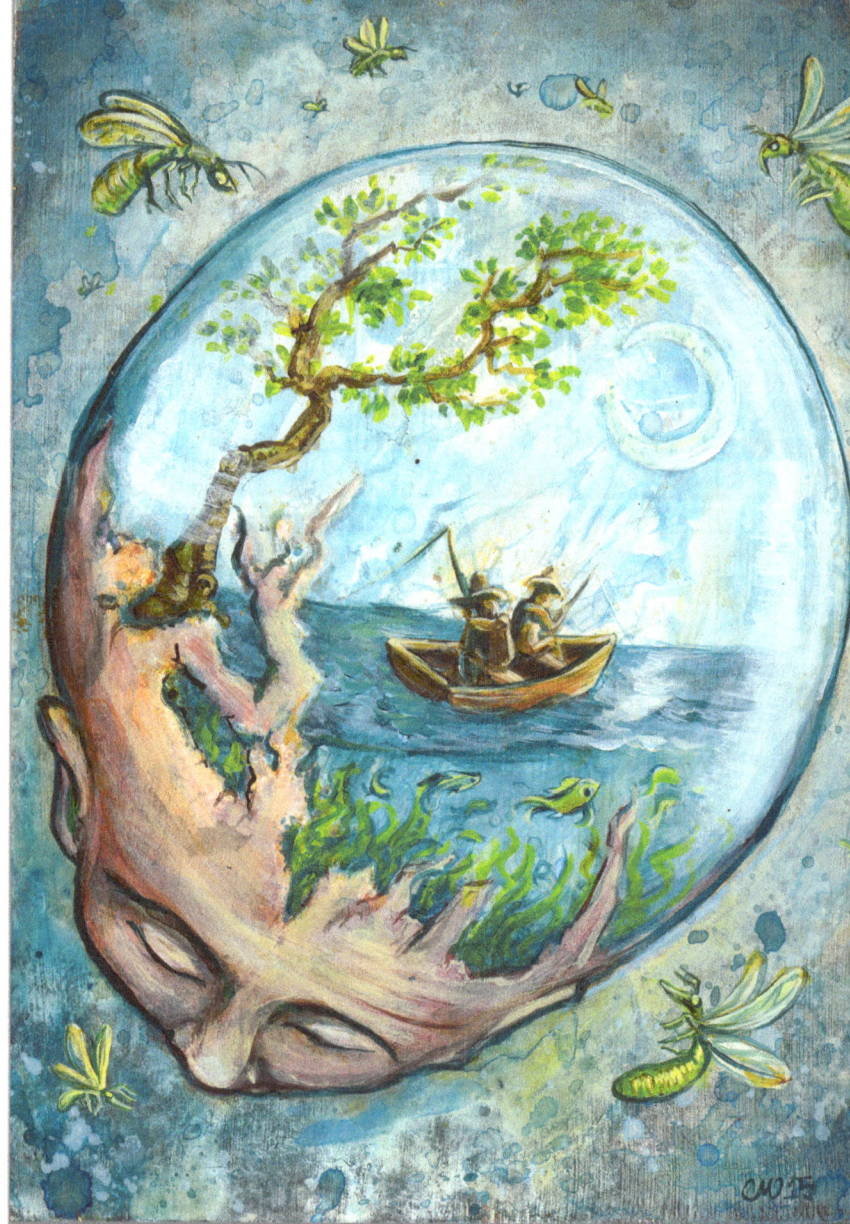

The Mosquitoes Arent What We Remembered 9"x12"

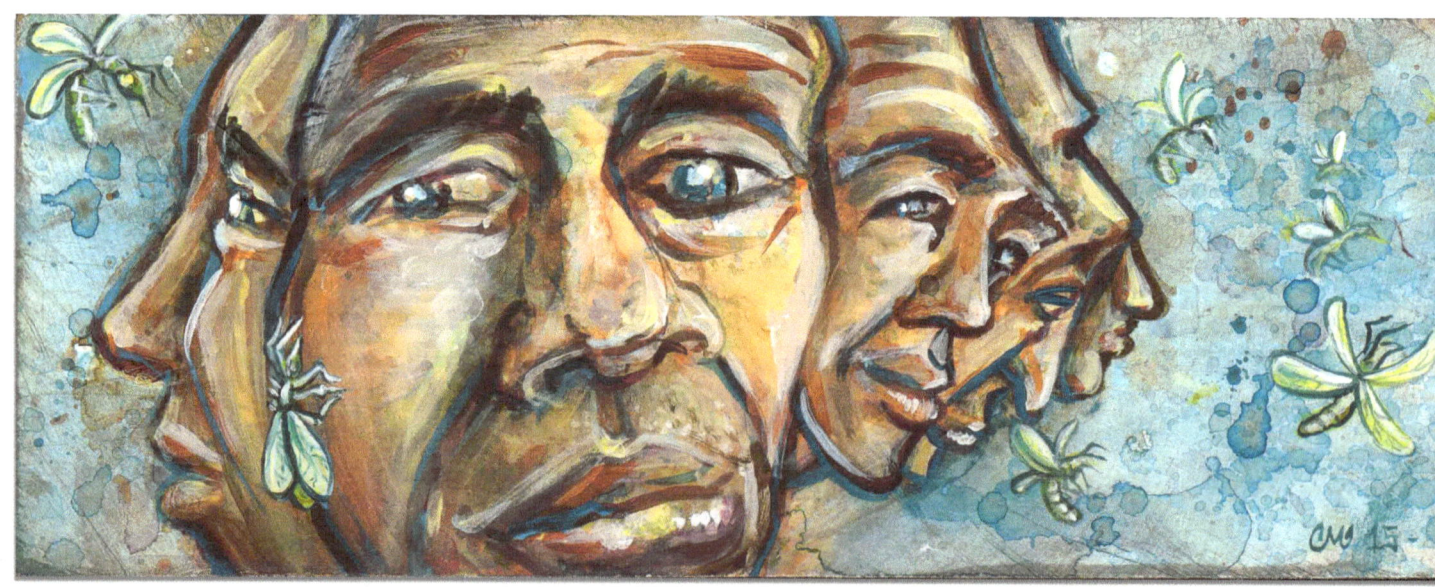

Where We Choose To Focus 3"x8"

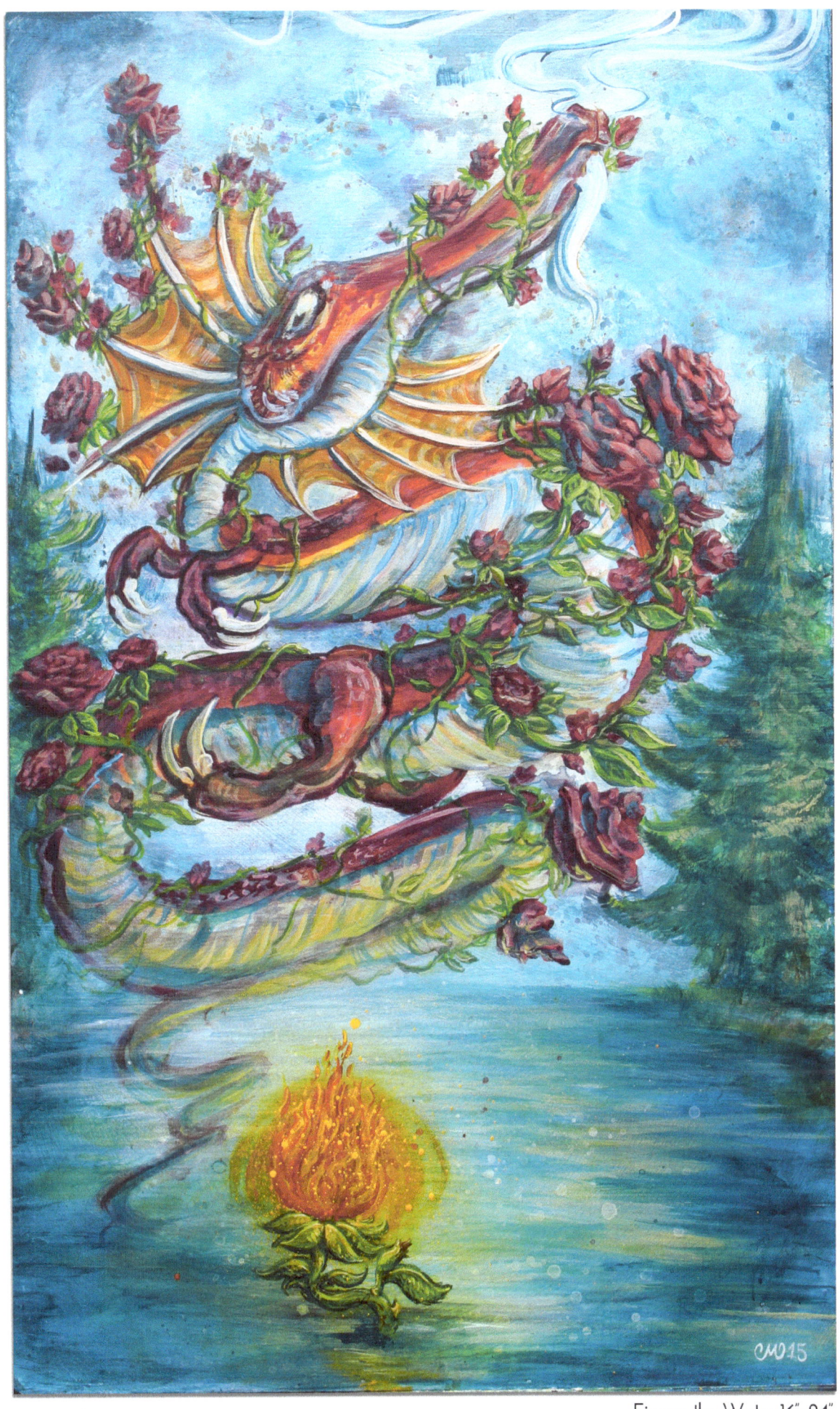

Fire on the Water 16"x24"

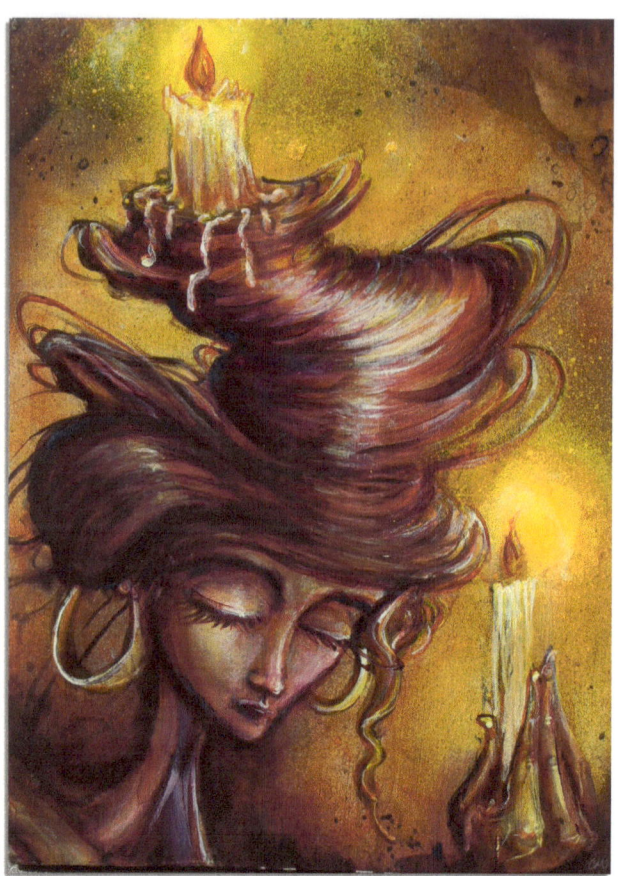

Insight 9"x12"

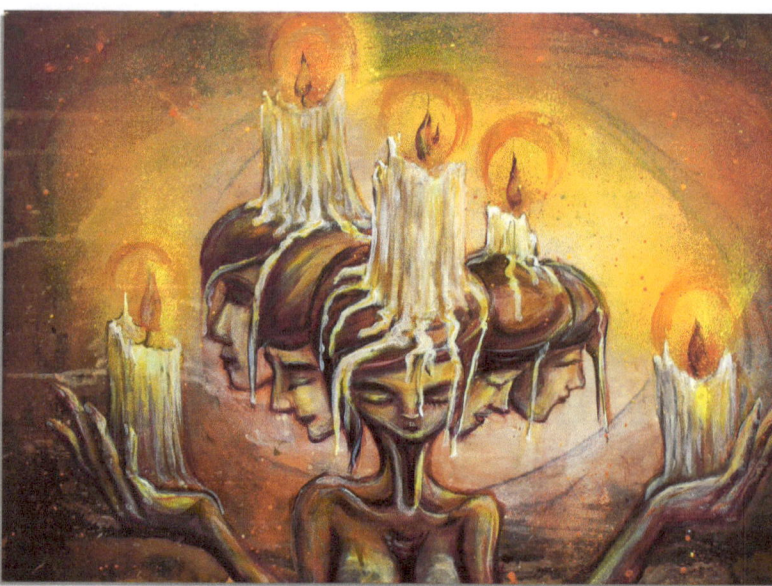

Insight at Hand 16"x24"

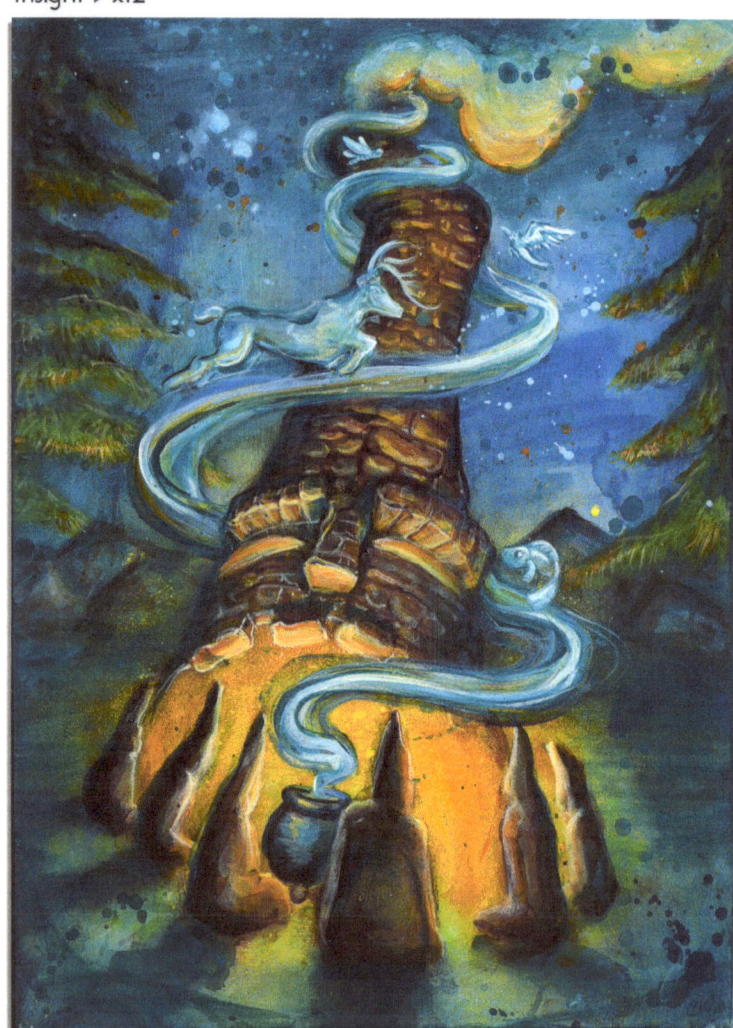

Covenant 9"x12"

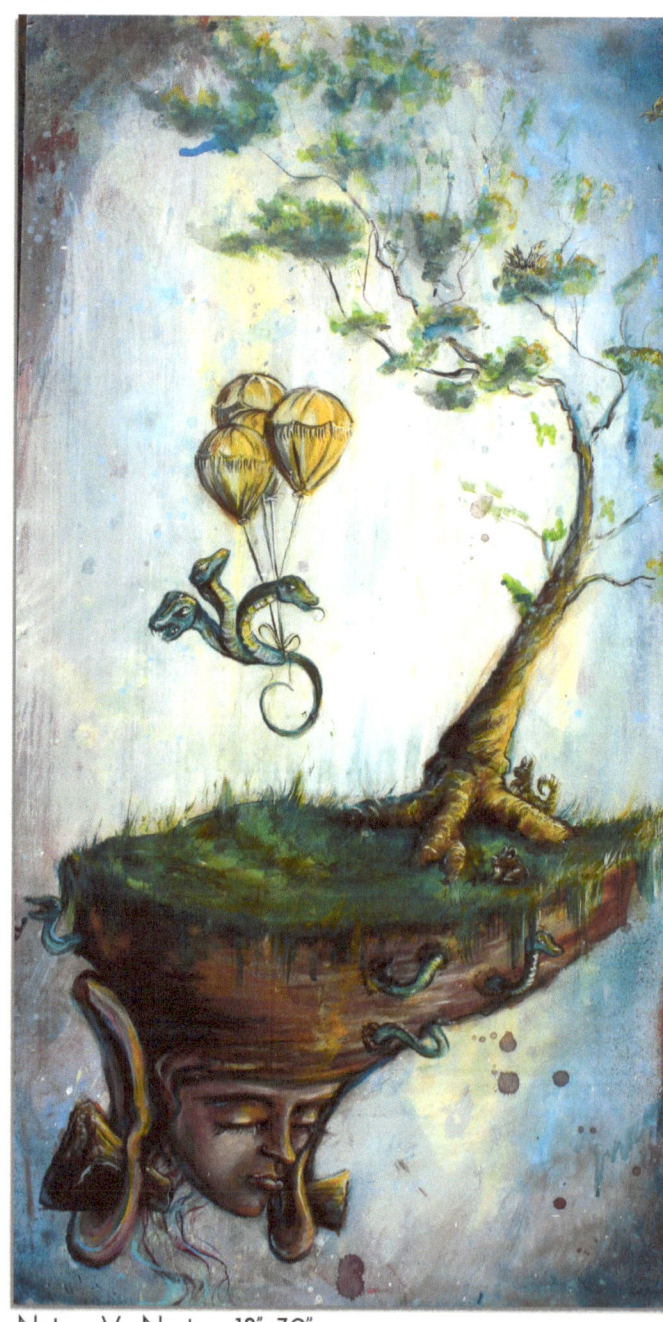

Nature Vs. Nurture 18"x30"

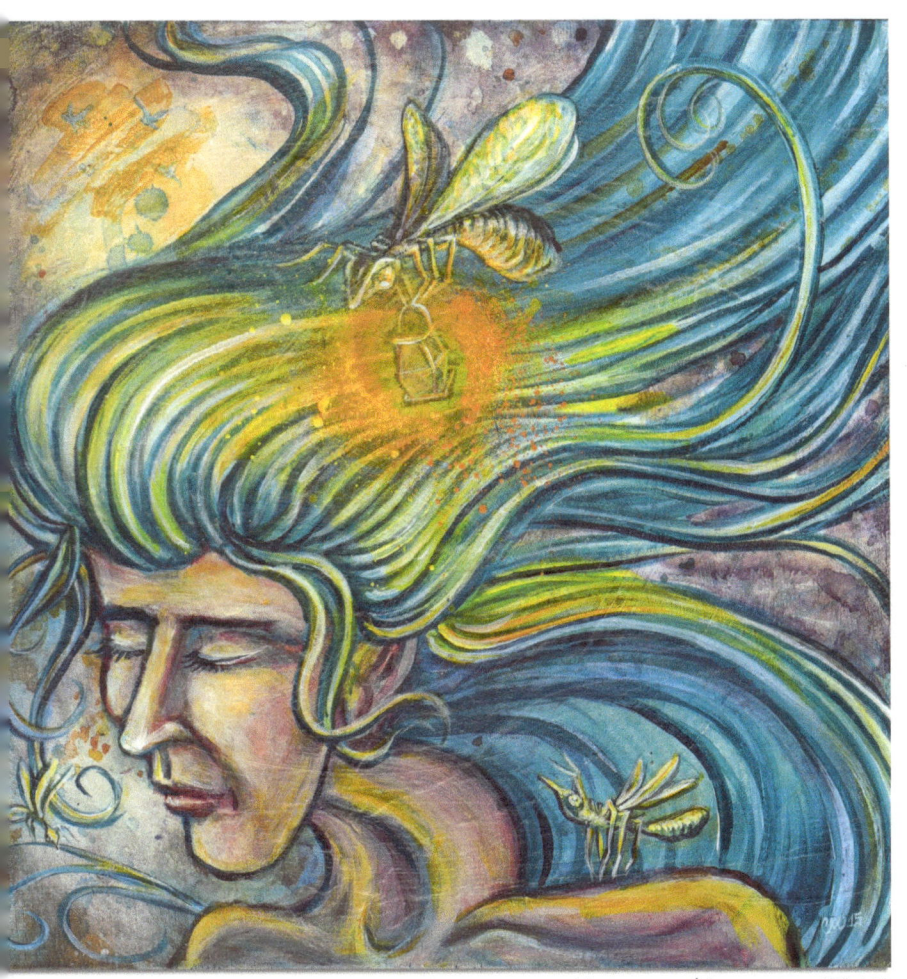

Settlement Entwined 18"x24"
Collaboration with Matt Schlosky

Unexpected Inspiration 12"x12"

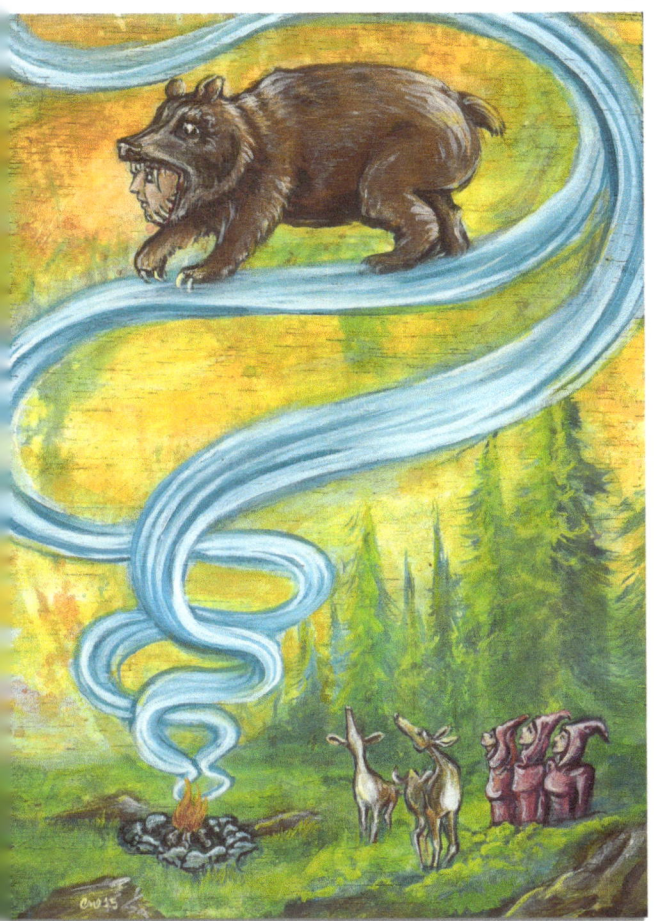

I Think You'd Like Me If You Got To Know Me 9"x12"

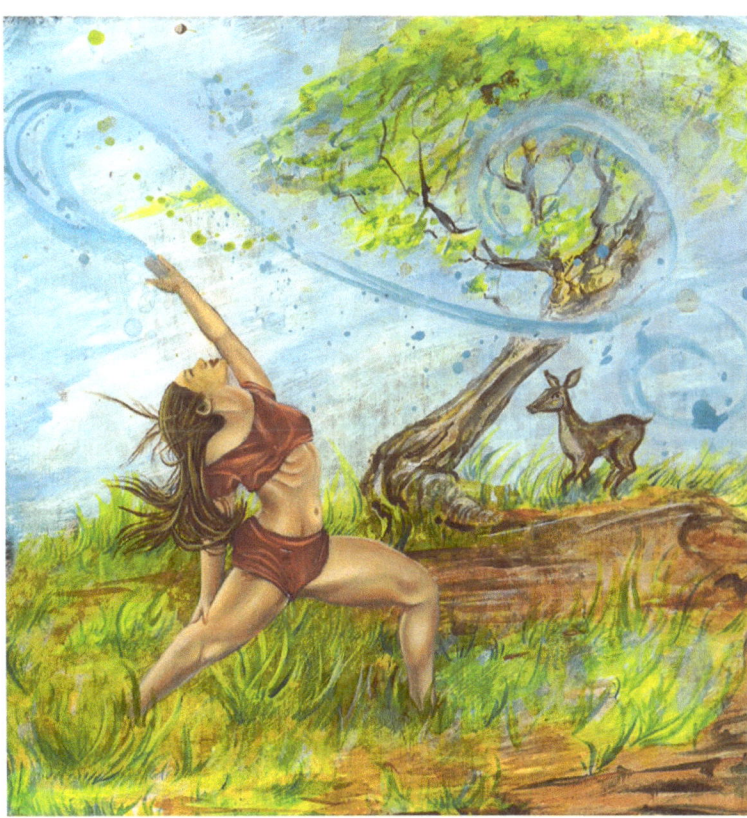

Warrior Pose 12"x12" Collaboration with Jen Griffo

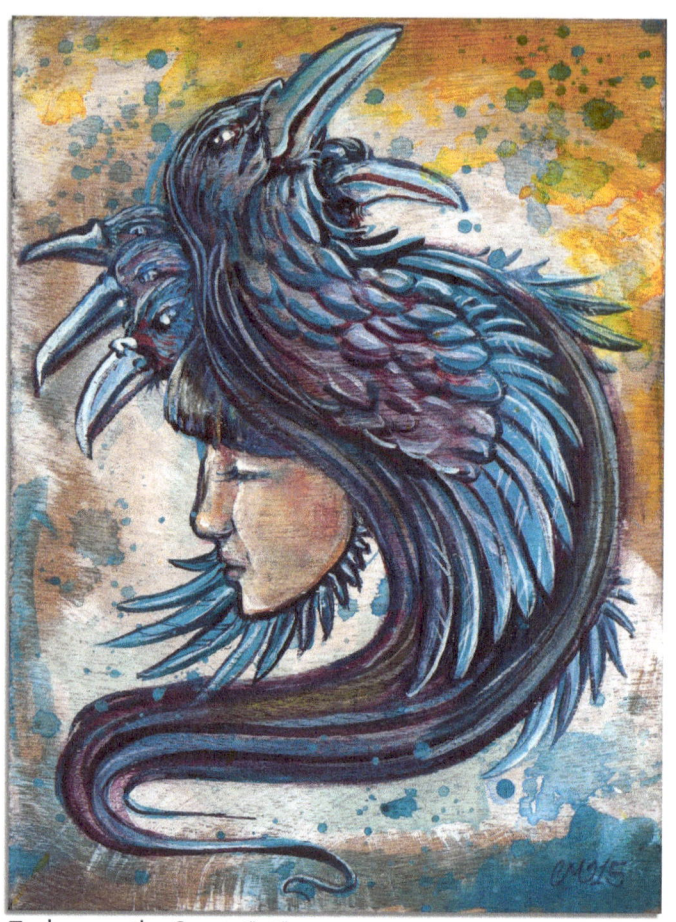

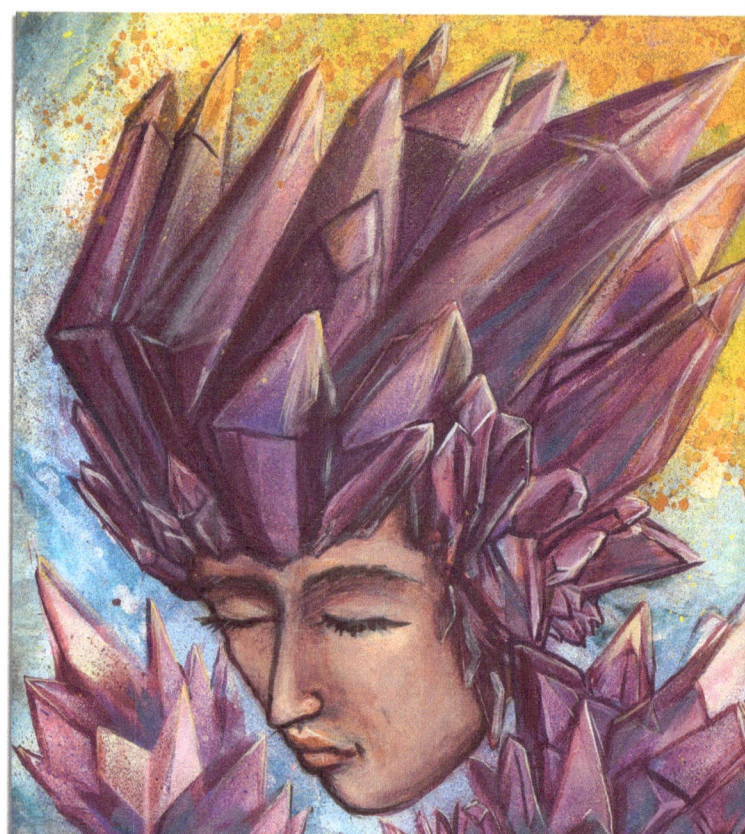

Crystalline 12"x12"

Embracing the Spirit 6"x9"

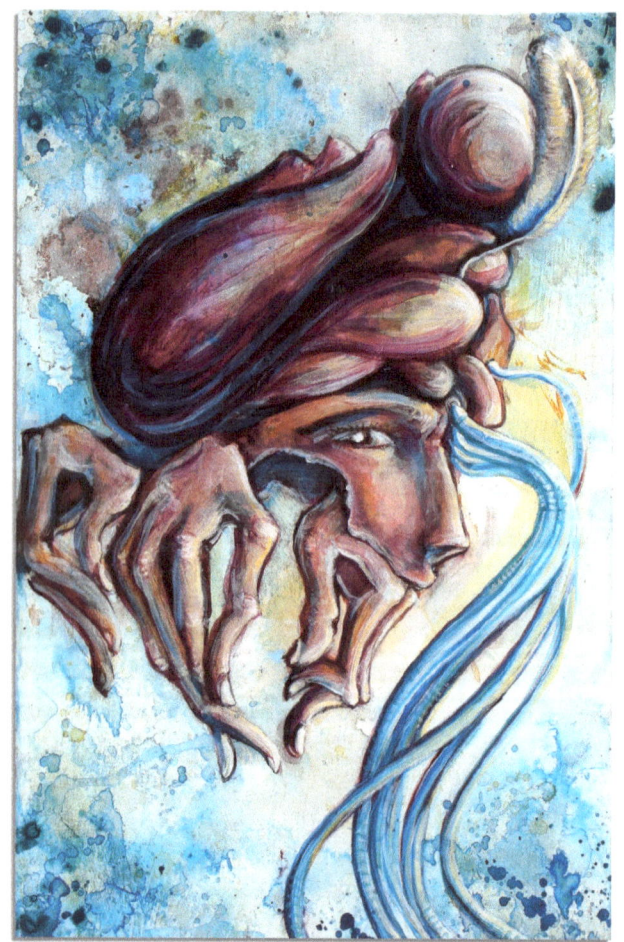

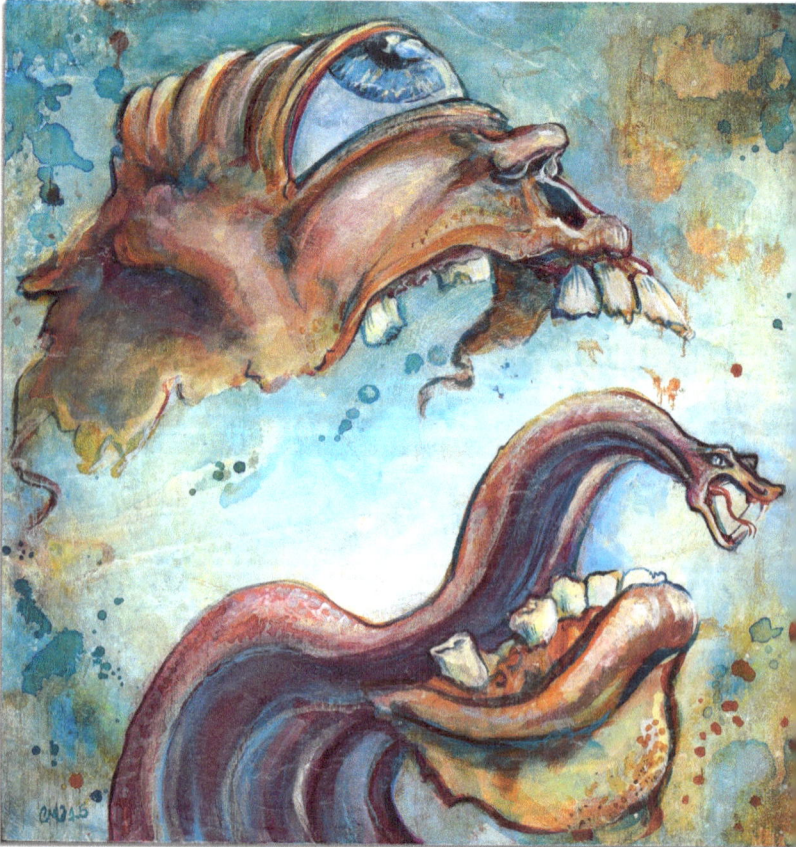

Divine Right 12"x16"

The Cyclops of Such-N-Such With a Serpent Tongue 12"x12"

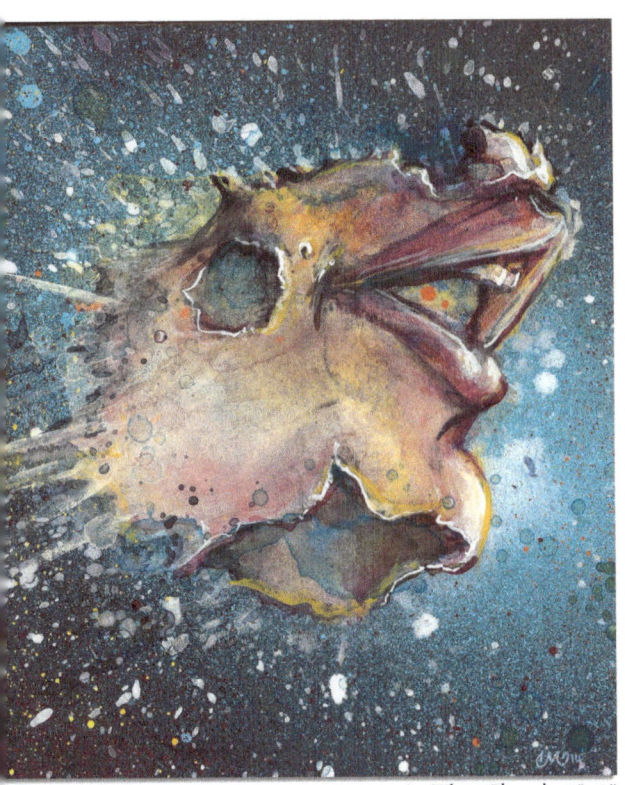

In The Clouds 8"x8"

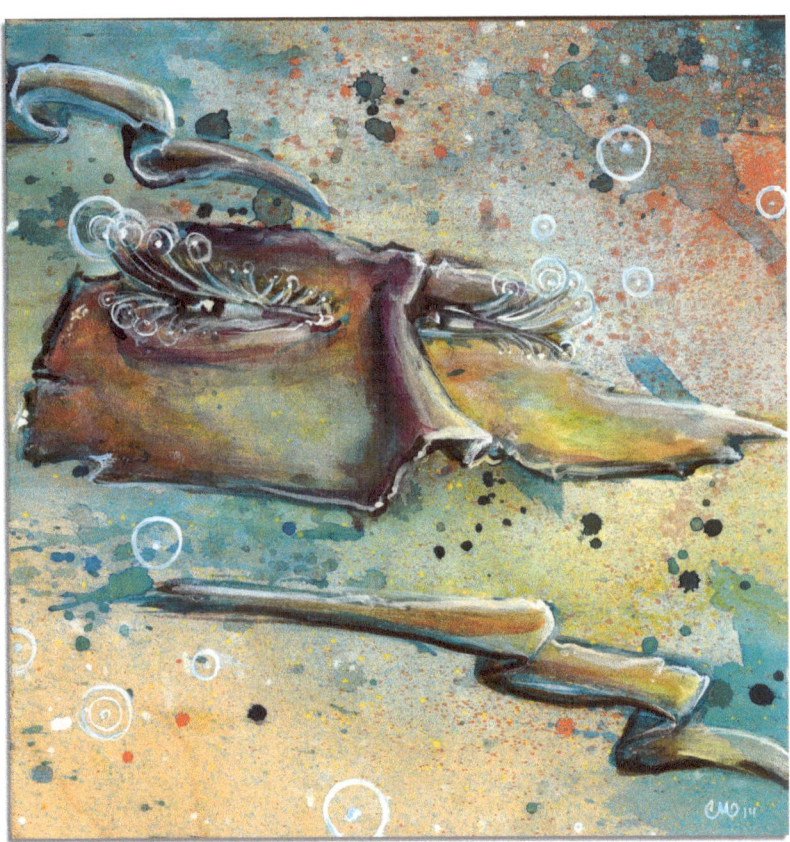

In The Clouds 8"x8"

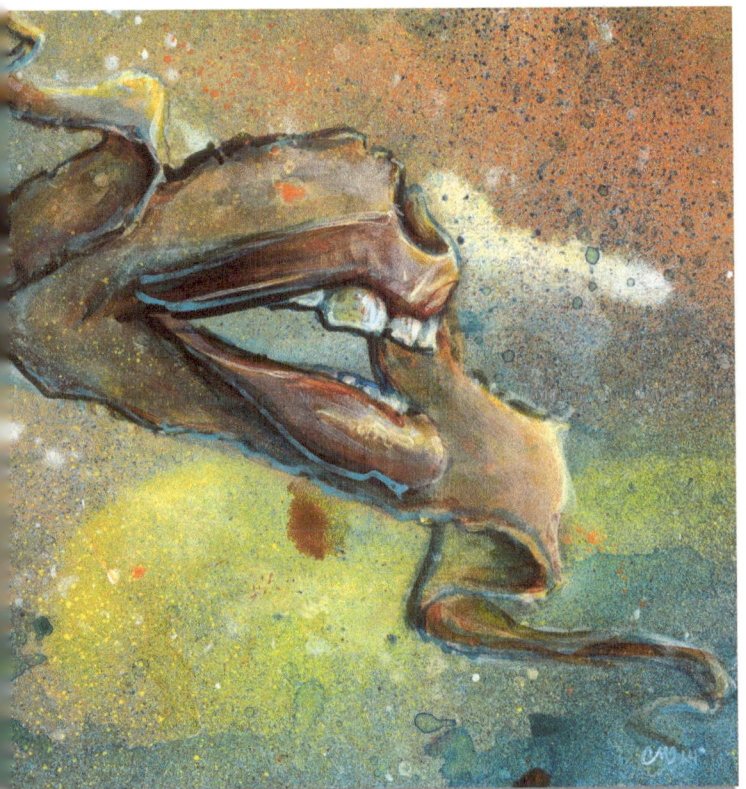

In the Clouds 8"x8"

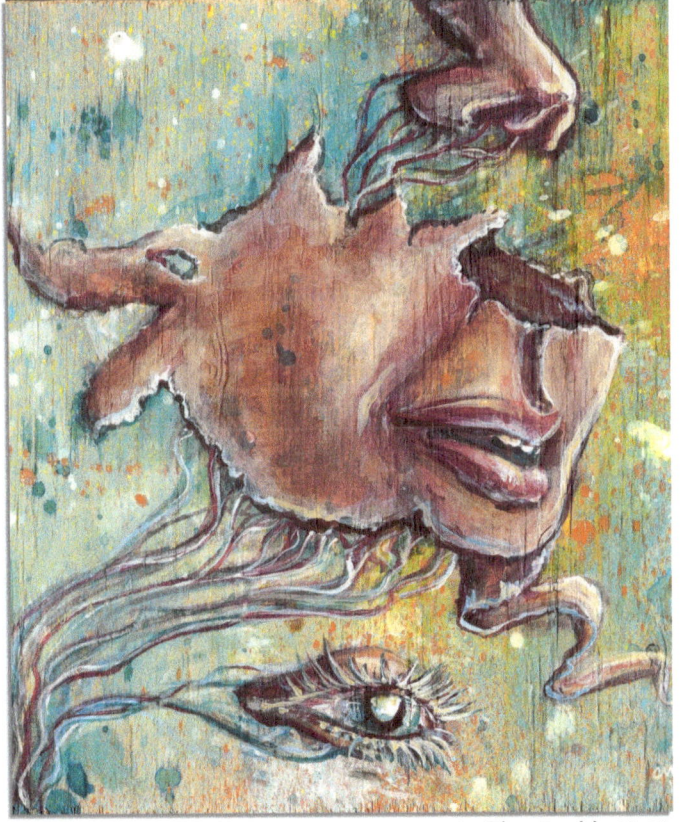

In The Coulds 8"x8"

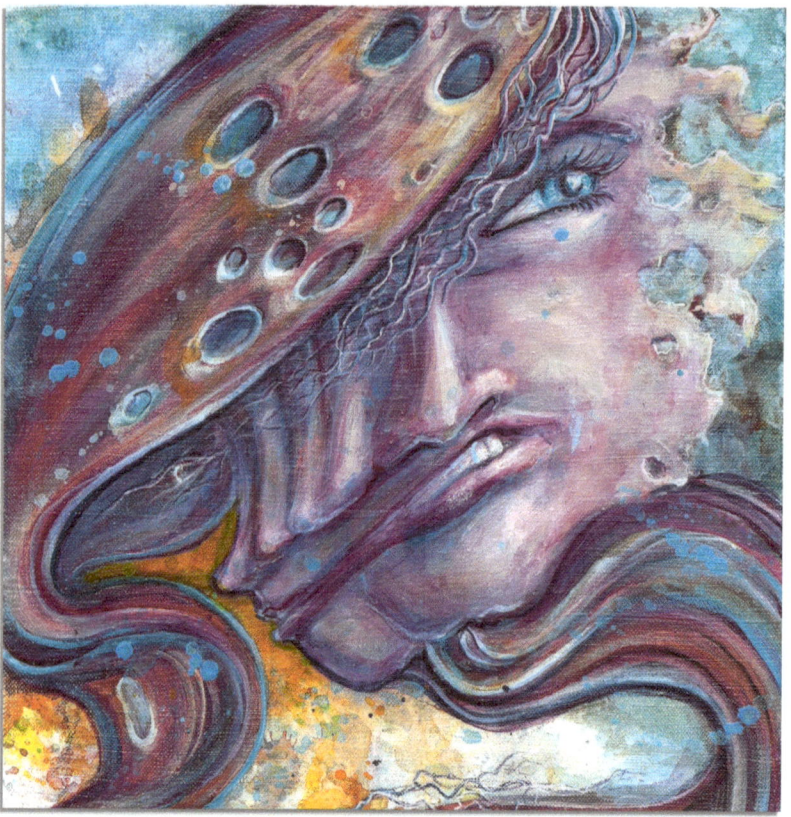

Were We Here Once? 12"x18"

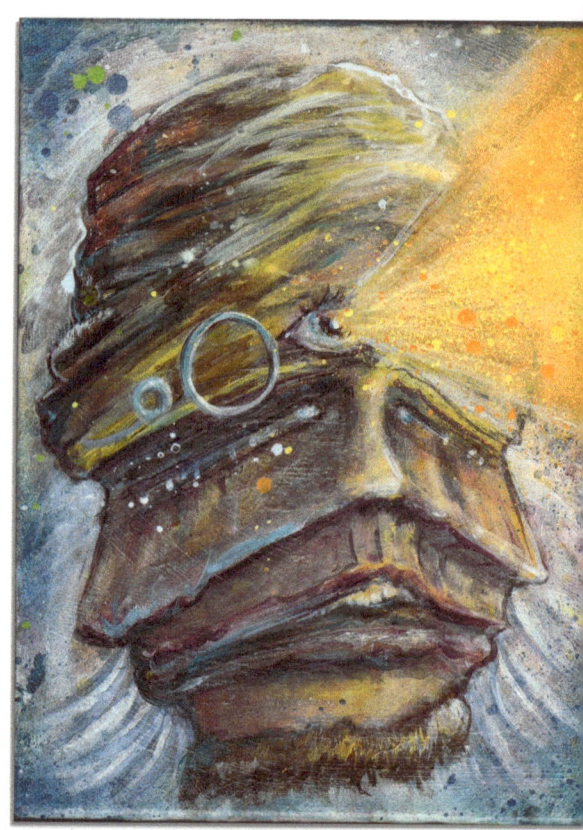

Steady Goes The First Eye 9"x12"

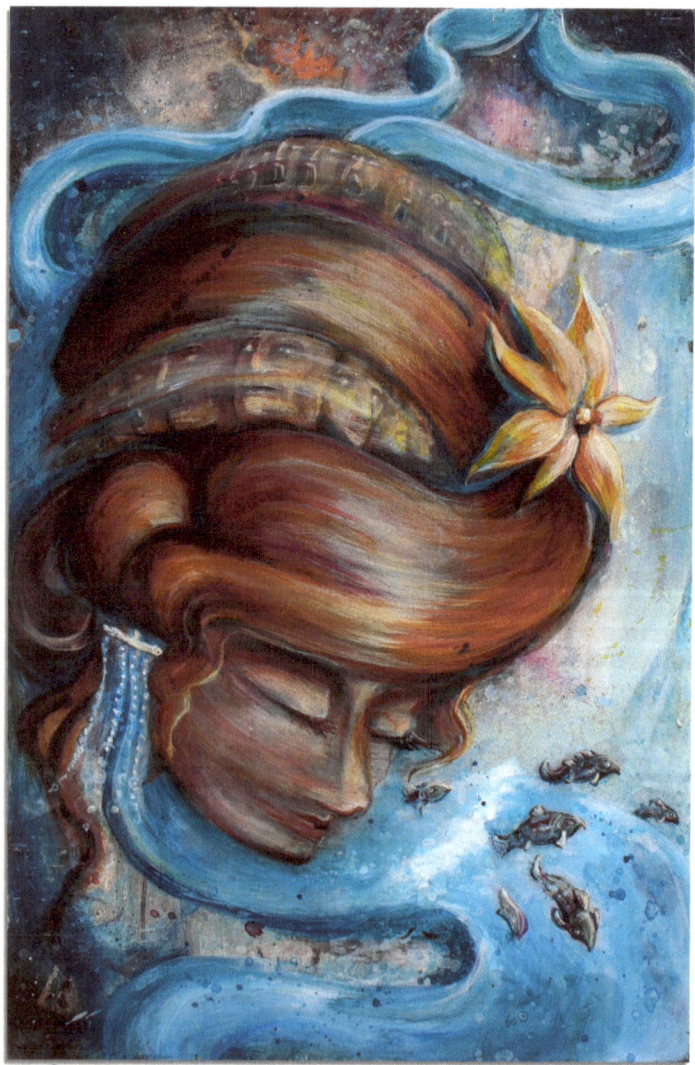

Perfect Hair Forever 18"x24"

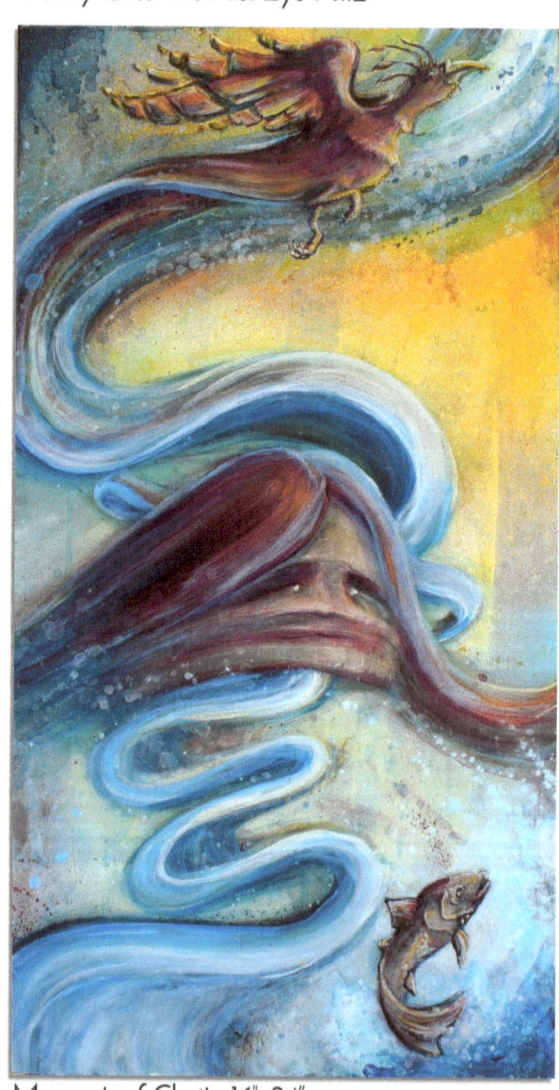

Moments of Clarity 16"x24"

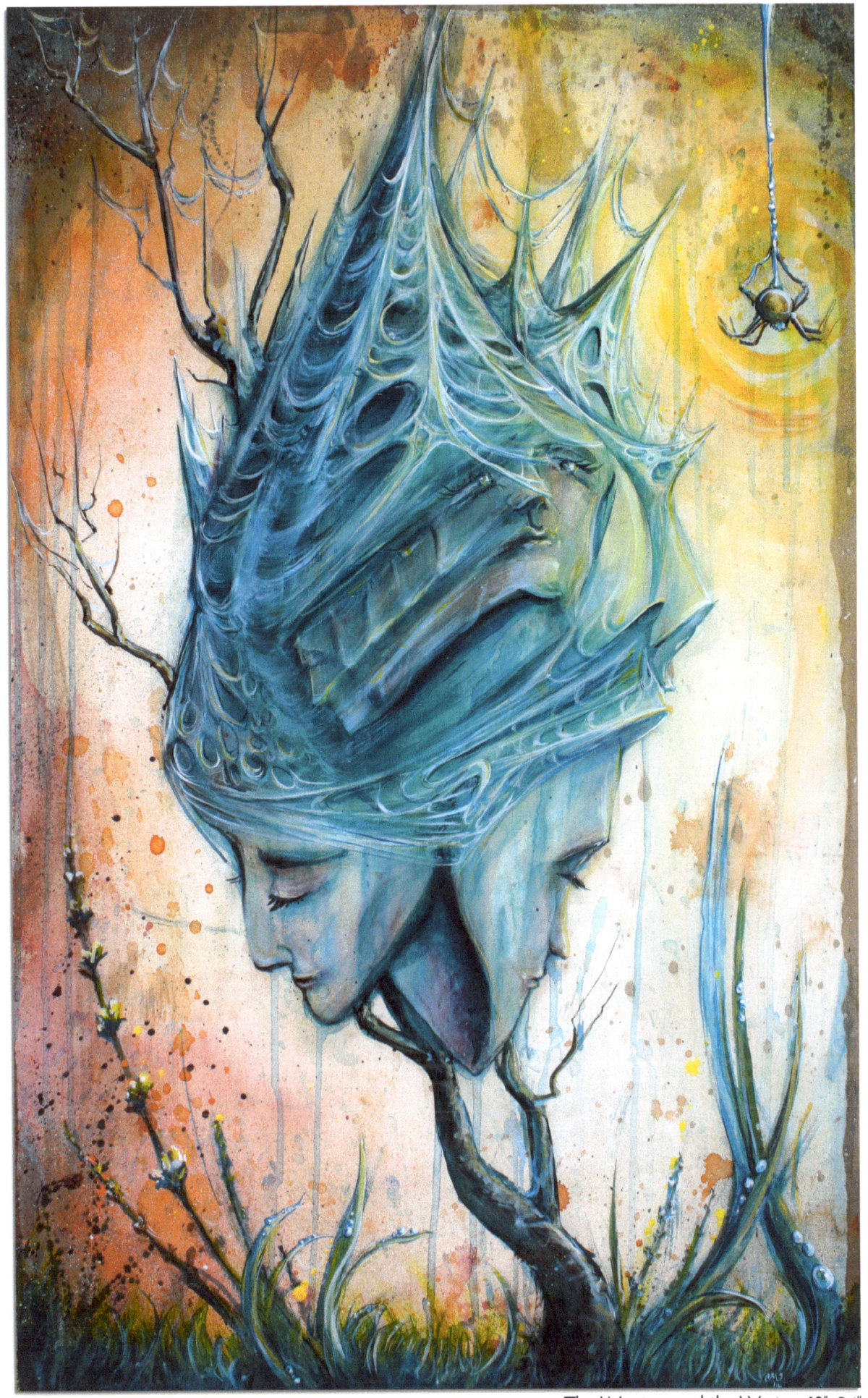

The Wanting and the Waiting 18"x24"

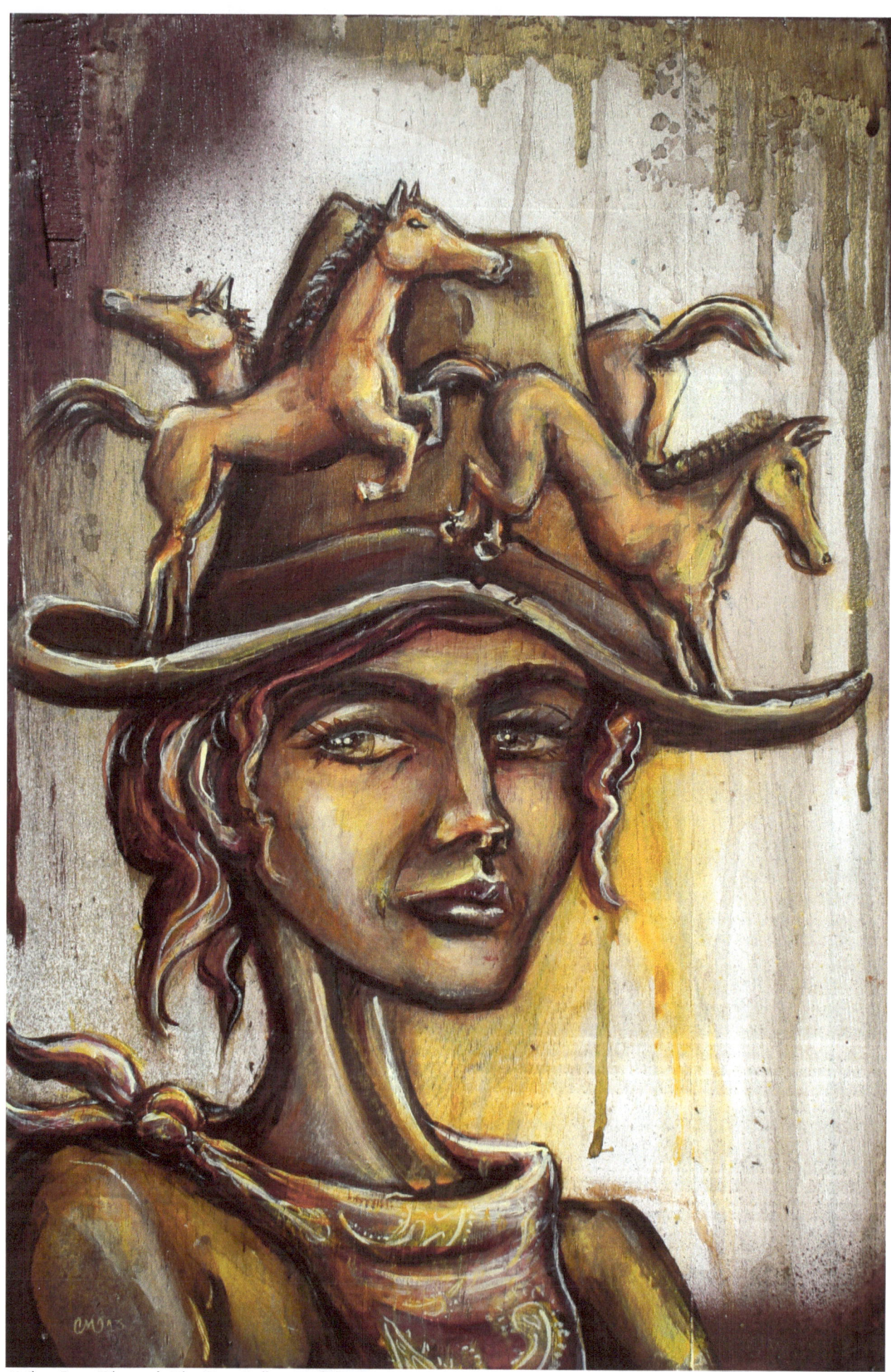

What Runs Through The Ten Gallon Hat? 12"x16"

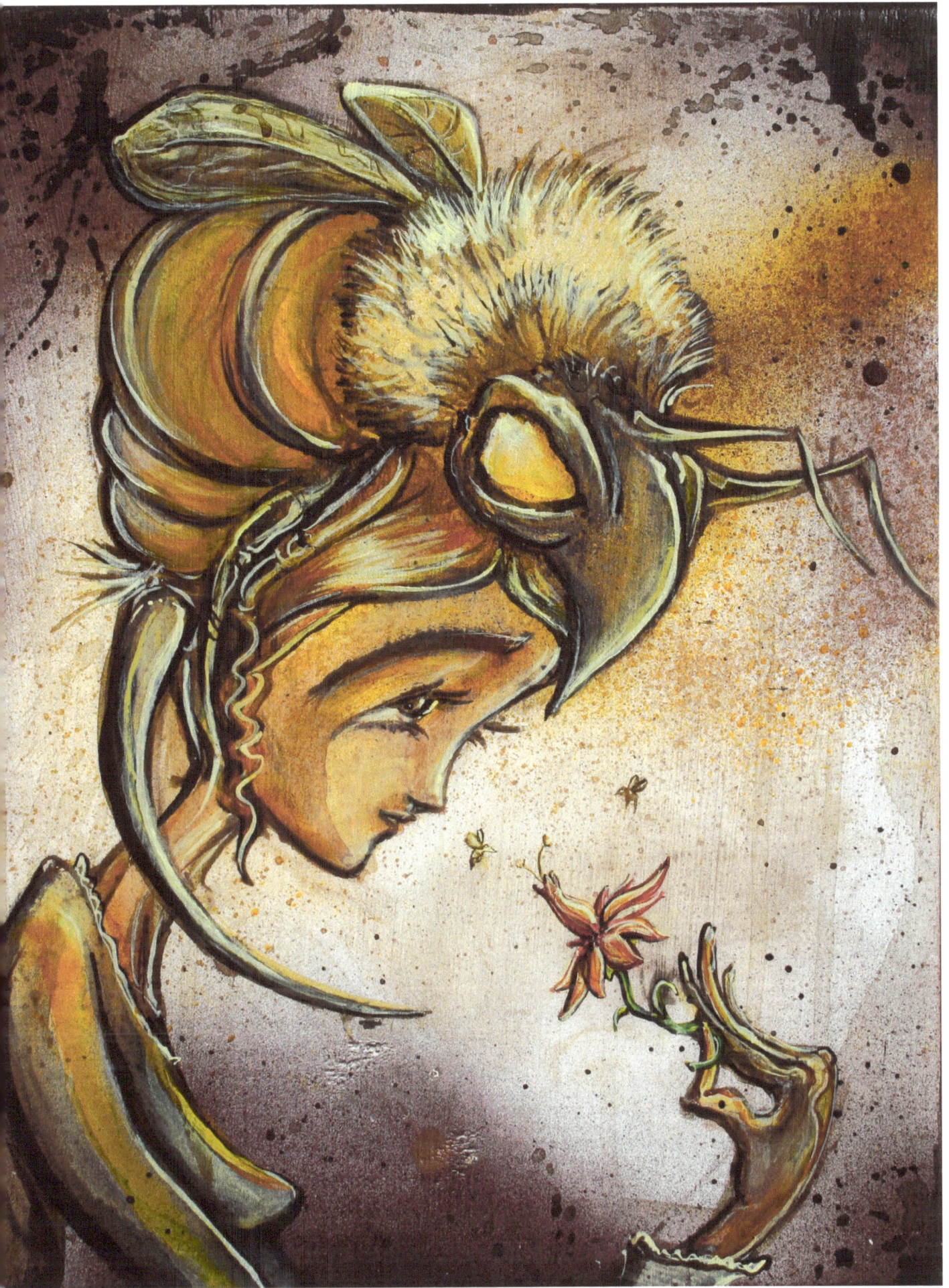

Making Friends 9"x12"

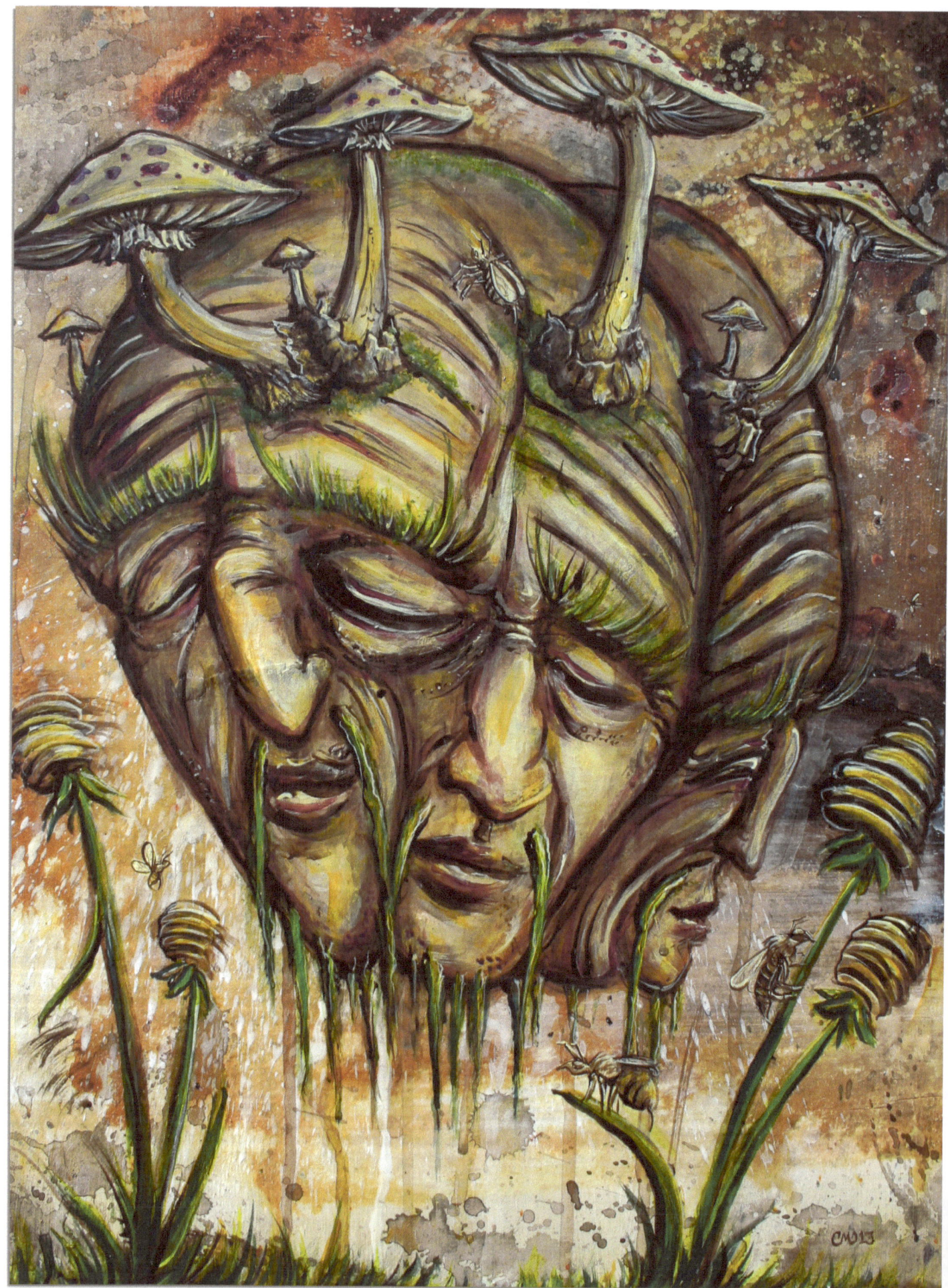

Hivemind 10"x14"

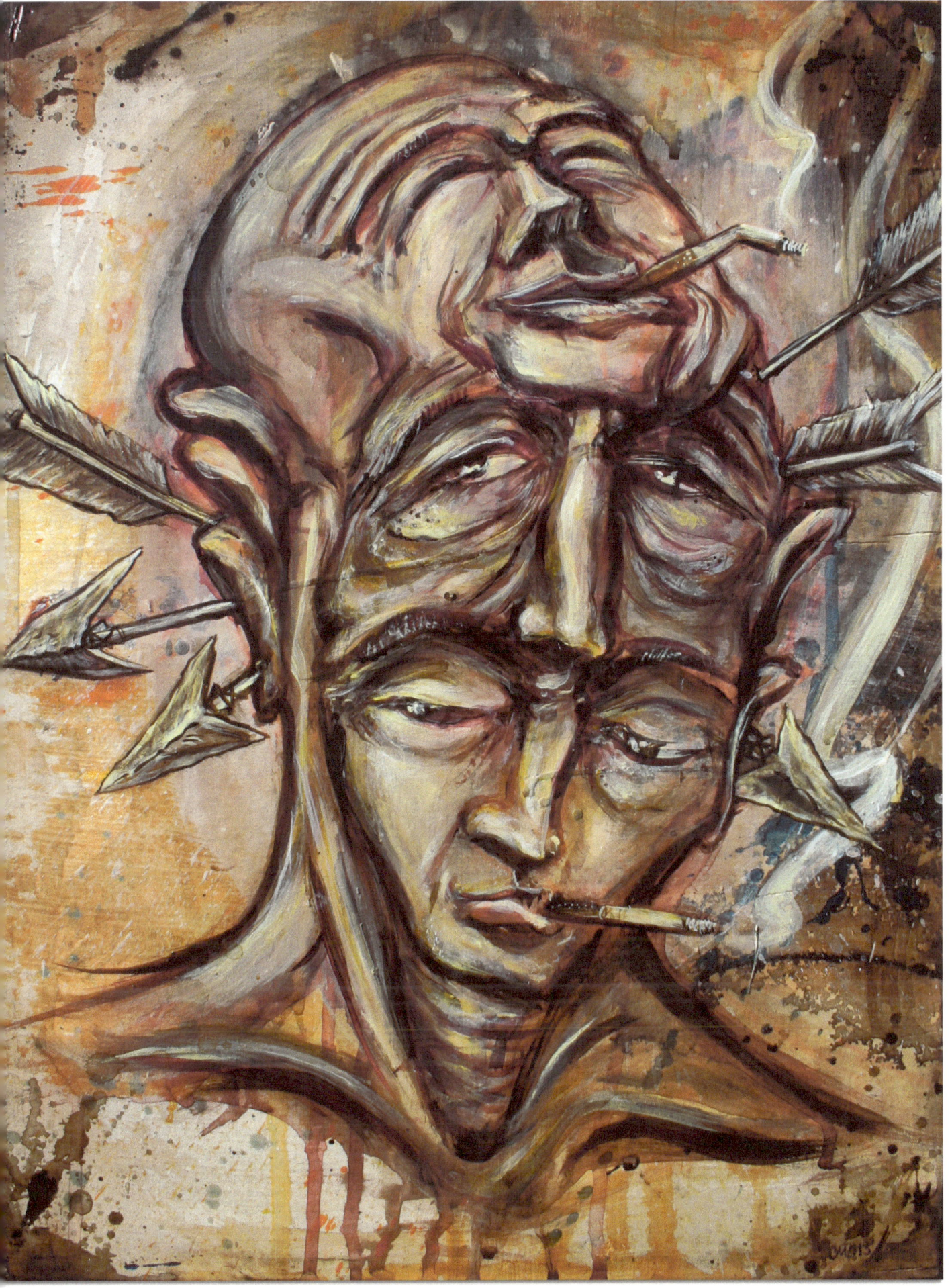

Perspective 10"x14"

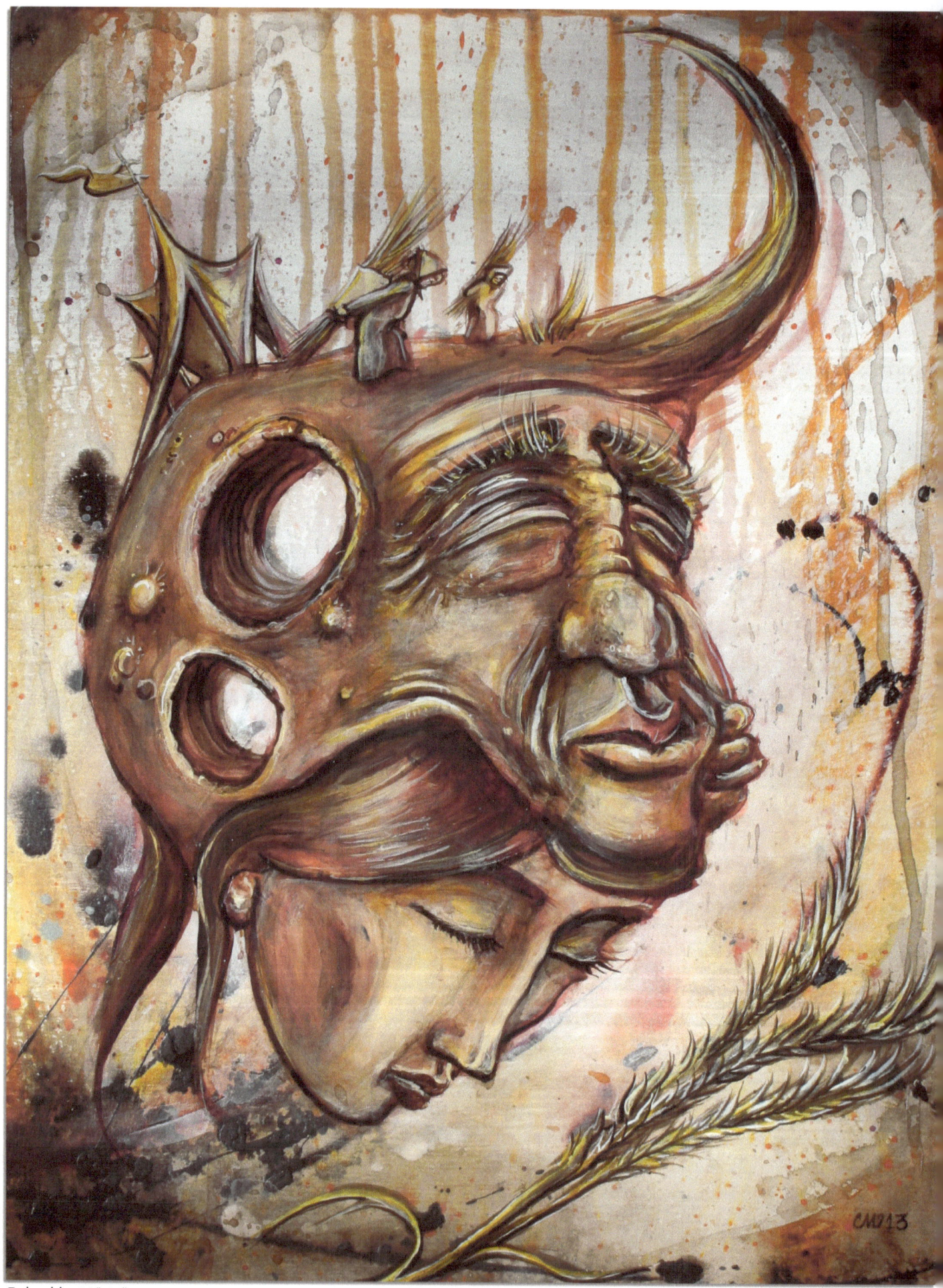

Babushka 10"x14"

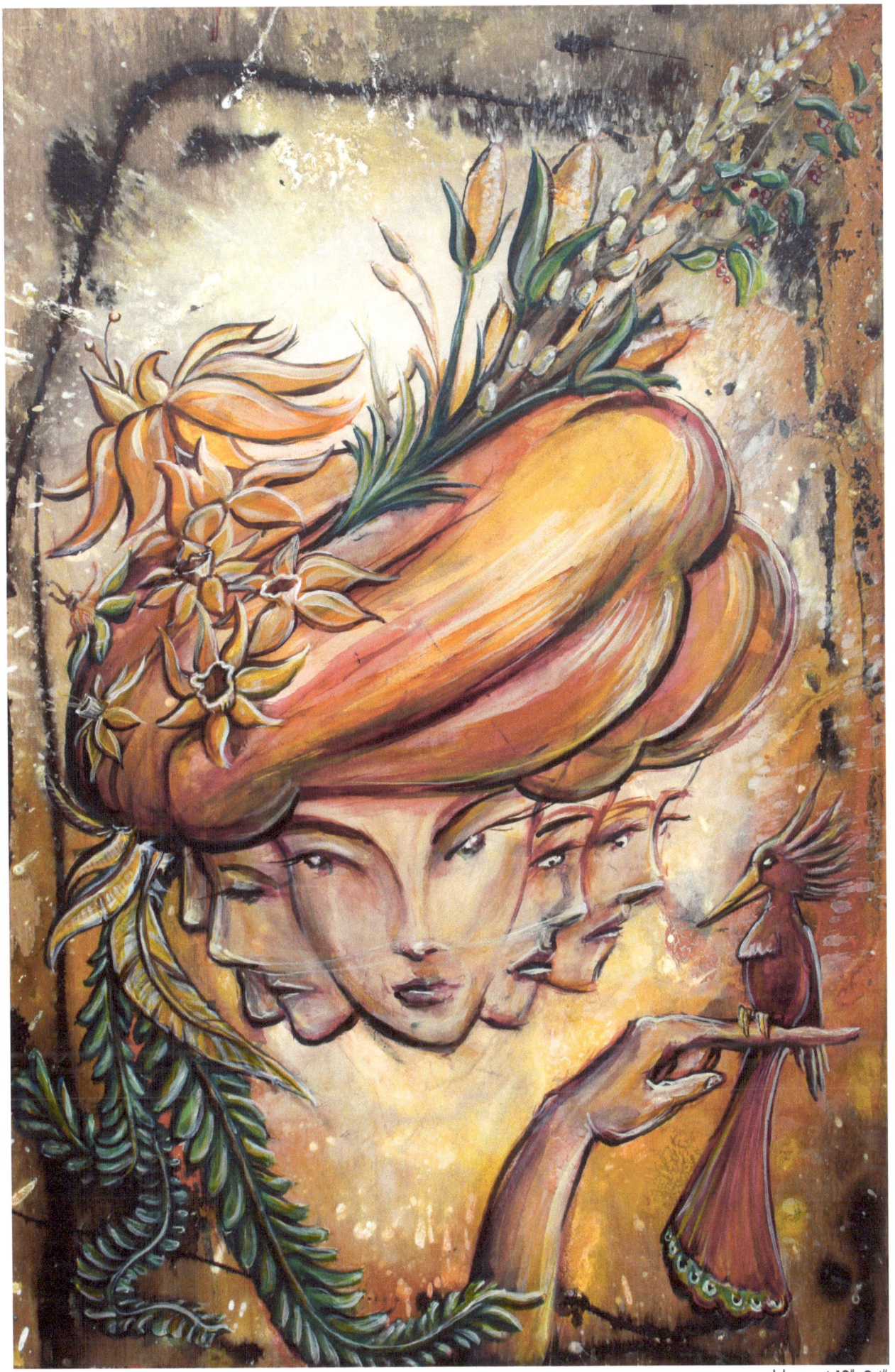

Harvest 18"x24"

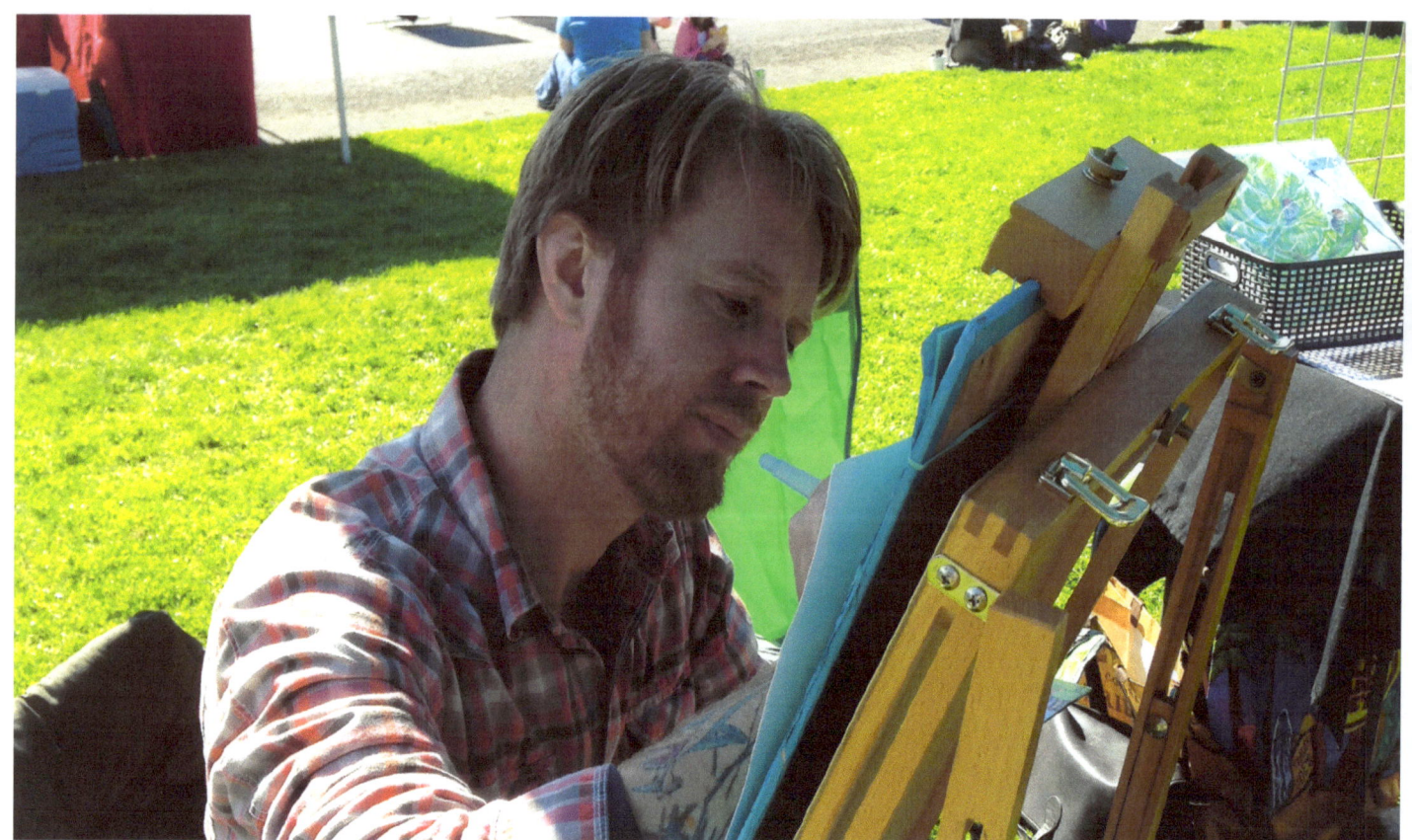

The majority of the paintings in this book were created in 2014 and 2015 with spray paint and acrylic, in Portland Oregon. My paintings are a deeply personal reflection of the world, that I don't know if I'll ever fully understand. Which is why I value other people's insight and interpretations, as this has lead to many personal revelations. Painting has been very therapeutic for me, helping me to learn, digest, and grow from personal trials, and to help comprehend the sometimes strange world we live in. For years the paintings I produced focused on social commentary, in an attempt to create a dialog, or inspire thought and emotion. After much personal exploration and growth, my work has evolved to focus on the what inspires me and brings me joy. As I recognize the woes of the world aren't going anywhere, and would like to promote positive change. I still have the intention of holding mirror to the world, but truly believe we need positive reinforcement, and solutions, to help us to unite, and be appreciative. If we always focus on injustice and hypocrisy, we miss the exquisitely chaotic, breathtaking beauty of the world we are lucky enough to be immersed in.

Thank you for taking a look, I hope you liked the book!

You can find me online at

www.Catastropher.com

www.ingramcontent.com/pod-product-compliance
Lightning Source LLC
Chambersburg PA
CBHW050905180526
45159CB00007B/2798